Introduction

In my experience, many people who fancy themselves investors know more about selecting a new flat-screen television or living room couch than about buying stocks! That's mind-boggling when you consider the enormous impact—positive or negative—that stock investing can have on your finances and your future.

You're already beyond that—after all, you bought this book. Maybe you want to choose and manage your own portfolio of stocks. Or maybe you're just curious about how stocks and investing work. Either way, you've come to the right place.

I'll start by making sure you understand the basics of how stocks and markets work. I'll talk in plain language about different investment strategies and why each of them has its appeal. You'll learn how to research, buy, sell, and track individual stocks—and how to create an overall portfolio that meets your financial goals.

If you're expecting inside tips, magical formulas, or mega-trend forecasts, this isn't the book for you. But if you're ready for a logical, methodical approach to markets, stocks, and the businesses behind them, keep reading.

Who am I to tell you all this? Well, I've been selecting and managing stocks for more than 20 years. As the chief investment officer at two major mutual-fund companies, I've been responsible for portfolios worth billions of dollars.

I like to joke that being in the investment business gave me an excuse for reading three newspapers a day. It also made me a great conversationalist at parties: no matter what someone said they did for a living, I could follow up with an intelligent question or comment about their industry.

I hope this book will equip you to ask intelligent questions about investments, and find intelligent answers, too. Even if you never buy a stock yourself, understanding stocks and markets can help you better manage your retirement and other investment accounts. If you're already managing a portfolio of stocks—or plan to—it's knowledge you simply can't afford to be without.

—Theresa Hamacher, CFA

Extras

In addition to the main text, this book includes four kinds of sidebars, each with a distinctive visual cue:

 Market Speak

Here you'll find definitions of common stock and investing terms.

 Red Flags

If you see these, look sharp! This sidebar warns you of things *not* to do.

THE POCKET IDIOT'S GUIDE™ TO

Investing in Stocks

by Theresa Hamacher, CFA,
Randy Burgess, and Carl Baldassarre

A member of Penguin Group (USA) Inc.

ALPHA BOOKS

Published by the Penguin Group

Penguin Group (USA) Inc., 375 Hudson Street, New York, New York 10014, USA

Penguin Group (Canada), 90 Eglinton Avenue East, Suite 700, Toronto, Ontario M4P 2Y3, Canada (a division of Pearson Penguin Canada Inc.)

Penguin Books Ltd., 80 Strand, London WC2R 0RL, England

Penguin Ireland, 25 St. Stephen's Green, Dublin 2, Ireland (a division of Penguin Books Ltd.)

Penguin Group (Australia), 250 Camberwell Road, Camberwell, Victoria 3124, Australia (a division of Pearson Australia Group Pty. Ltd.)

Penguin Books India Pvt. Ltd., 11 Community Centre, Panchsheel Park, New Delhi—110 017, India

Penguin Group (NZ), 67 Apollo Drive, Rosedale, North Shore, Auckland 1311, New Zealand (a division of Pearson New Zealand Ltd.)

Penguin Books (South Africa) (Pty.) Ltd., 24 Sturdee Avenue, Rosebank, Johannesburg 2196, South Africa

Penguin Books Ltd., Registered Offices: 80 Strand, London WC2R 0RL, England

Copyright © 2006 by Penguin Group (USA) Inc.

THE POCKET IDIOT'S GUIDE TO and Design are trademarks of Penguin Group (USA) Inc.

International Standard Book Number: 978-1-59257-473-5

Library of Congress Catalog Card Number: 2005935928

15   14   13   10   9

Interpretation of the printing code: The rightmost number of the first series of numbers is the year of the book's printing; the rightmost number of the second series of numbers is the number of the book's printing. For example, a printing code of 06-1 shows that the first printing occurred in 2006.

Printed in the United States of America

Note: This publication contains the opinions and ideas of its authors. It is intended to provide helpful and informative material on the subject matter covered. It is sold with the understanding that the authors and publisher are not engaged in rendering professional services in the book. If the reader requires personal assistance or advice, a competent professional should be consulted.

The authors and publisher specifically disclaim any responsibility for any liability, loss, or risk, personal or otherwise, which is incurred as a consequence, directly or indirectly, of the use and application of any of the contents of this book.

Most Alpha books are available at special quantity discounts for bulk purchases for sales promotions, premiums, fund-raising, or educational use. Special books, or book excerpts, can also be created to fit specific needs.

For details, write: Special Markets, Alpha Books, 375 Hudson Street, New York, NY 10014.

Contents

Appendixes

Contents

Bulls & Bears _____

These give you short quotes from great stock-picking minds such as Peter Lynch and Warren Buffett, as well as from other assorted experts.

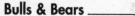 **The Bottom Line** _____

These contain tips and extra information not found in the text.

Acknowledgments

The authors would like to thank Elizabeth Watson for her expert answers to our questions about securities laws and regulations.

We also want to thank our families and friends for their unceasing support in the face of long hours and tight deadlines. This goes double for our significant others—Greg, Marian, and Katherine—as well as for Carl's two daughters, Marie and Juliana, who have the makings of fine investors already.

Trademarks

All terms mentioned in this book that are known to be or are suspected of being trademarks or service marks have been appropriately capitalized. Alpha Books and Penguin Group (USA) Inc. cannot attest to the accuracy of this information. Use of a term in this book should not be regarded as affecting the validity of any trademark or service mark.

Why Stocks?

In This Chapter

- The case for stocks
- Do it yourself or outsource
- Myths versus realities
- Setting goals

Back in the days of your grandparents and even your parents, owning stocks was harder than it is today. Costs were high, and mutual funds few and far between. So the skill to pick stocks was essential: either you or your broker had to decide when and what to buy and sell. Owning a stock meant learning its trading symbol, and sometimes owning an actual paper certificate.

But today, you don't have to pick stocks at all to own literally hundreds of them. Instead, all you have to do is invest in one of the many low-cost, tax-efficient mutual funds that track the market as a whole. These so-called "index funds" make investing in the stock market a breeze.

So are there any reasons to still pick stocks? You bet.

First, stock-picking gives you a shot at doing better than the index funds. The market can have a good year, but you can have a great year. Or the market can have a terrible year, but you can have a not-so-bad year. Sure, you can also do worse than the market—but there are ways to manage this risk, as you'll find out. Second, it's a great way to learn more about managing your personal finances in general, including retirement accounts and your other big investments. Third, stock-picking today is easier than ever, thanks to low commissions, online trading, and a plethora of research tools. You can even argue that all this technology makes it more important, not less, to understand stocks and funds.

Finally, stock-picking is flexible. You can spend a lot of time each day on your stocks, just like a professional money manager—to the point you might even earn your living at it. Or you can own just a few stocks in addition to your mutual funds, making it a weekend hobby like woodworking or gardening.

Not sure whether you want to invest in stocks? Keep reading. Even if you decide to stick with mutual funds, you'll have learned a lot about the stocks those funds consist of, and you'll make better decisions as a result.

In this opening chapter, we look at exactly why *stocks* are so attractive, especially when compared to other common investments such as bonds. We dispel some of the myths and exaggerations about stock-picking, and then talk about how to set your own investing goals. You'll have plenty to think about in just a few pages, so let's get started!

> ## ($) Market Speak _____
>
> **Stock** or **equity** is a share of owner-
> ship in a corporation. In fact, the
> term *equities* is often used in the investment
> industry as a synonym for "stocks."
> Technically, even a single share of stock
> makes you an owner and gives you a vote
> on how the business is run. In fact, though,
> large publicly traded firms such as IBM or
> Wal-Mart have millions of shares outstand-
> ing. Although a few big shots may own
> enough of those shares to actually influ-
> ence policy, you probably won't. What
> stock ownership really means to you is a
> share in the corporation's assets, future
> growth, and profits.

The Case for Stocks

Owning stocks is risky, takes work, and requires
ongoing attention. So what makes it all worth-
while? Simply this: stocks give you an opportunity
to share in the rich rewards that can come with
owning a business.

When you buy stock, you own a small part of the
business behind the shares. If that business grows and
prospers, your slice of the pie should expand, too.

For example, suppose you liked shopping at Home
Depot so much that, after doing some research,
you decided to buy 100 shares back in early 1996,
paying a little more than $1,000. If you'd held on,

your stake would have more than quadrupled, to $4,126 as of January 31, 2004.

During that same period, Home Depot's sales grew from $15 billion to $73 billion, and the number of stores the company operated grew from 423 to more than 1,800. Notice that the growth in sales and number of stores is fairly close to the growth in the stock value. As the company did well, it became more valuable, and your ownership stake was worth more.

The Bottom Line

How much can finding and holding on to a great stock be worth? Here's an example: If you'd bought 100 shares of Microsoft in 1986, on the first day the company offered stock to the public, you'd have paid about $2,100. Had you held that stock until December 31, 2004, reinvesting your dividends along the way, your holding would have grown to 28,800 shares, worth $770,000.

Stocks Offer Long-Term Growth

Although the growth of Home Depot's business and share price has been particularly good, it's hardly unprecedented. Let's take a longer time span and a broader sample. If you had invested just $1,000 in the largest stocks in the market in 1926 (the first year for which data is available), you'd have wound up with more than $2,500,000 by the end of 2004.

Sure, inflation accounted for some of that growth. Specifically, you'd need $10,600 at year-end 2004 to equal the buying power of $1,000 in 1926. That's a ten-fold difference. But our hypothetical stock investment didn't increase by a factor of 10—it increased by a factor of 2,500!

The real story here is the growth of the American economy over the past 80-odd years. Year after year, as the economy has grown, sales and profits for well-run companies have gone up, making them more valuable. Along the way, even the smallest stockholders have been amply rewarded.

No one knows what the future holds. But if you can find dynamic, profitable companies now, buying stock gives you an easy way to share in their potential growth.

Stocks Offer Short-Term Income and Tax Relief

There's another way stocks can repay investors: dividends. Dividends are a cash payment from a company to its shareholders. The amount is determined by the board of directors and varies widely from company to company.

Some companies pay no dividends at all, some pay relatively small amounts, and some pay considerably more. The average stock had a dividend yield of about 1.5 percent in 2004. At that rate, a share of stock worth $100 would pay a dividend of $1.50

per year. So if you owned 100 shares, you'd get $150 per year in dividends.

It's good to know you don't have to depend on a rising stock price alone to make money. If you can find well-run companies, dividends let you get a piece of their profits every year.

Although dividends are taxed as income every year, any growth in the value of stock shares is not—at least, not until you sell and realize a profit. When you do sell, the profits are taxed by the federal government at a top rate of just 15 percent, as long as you've owned the stock for at least a year. Compared to the top tax rate of 35 percent for salary income, that's a pretty good deal.

Stocks Versus Other Investments

Stocks are often compared with two other types of investments: bonds and cash. It's a natural comparison because stocks, bonds, and cash accounts all have something in common: they exist only on paper or in a computer's memory. You can buy and sell such paper assets quickly and inexpensively, when compared to tangible possessions such as houses and gold bars.

Still, bonds and cash are very different from stocks. To start with, bonds are really loans made by investors to corporations or governments, which then promise to repay you with interest. This makes bonds a more predictable investment than stocks, but because you're not an owner, it also means you won't share in a company's growth.

Cash is even simpler—it refers to the savings or money-market accounts almost everyone has. They're very safe. Accounts at banks are even insured by the government. Less risk means less reward, however, and cash accounts generally pay interest rates barely sufficient to keep your money a step ahead of inflation.

Stocks have generally fared well in comparison with both bonds and cash, as the following chart shows. Take our $1,000 investment in large-company stocks in 1926. As you saw, we'd have reaped a cool $2.5 million by the end of 2004. But what if we'd made that same investment, only in long-term U.S. government bonds? Our money would have grown to just $663,000. Investing it as cash would have hurt even more. We'd have wound up with a mere $18,000, only $7,400 ahead of inflation.

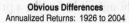

Obvious Differences
Annualized Returns: 1926 to 2004

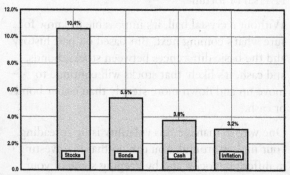

Stock returns easily outpaced those for bonds or cash in the 75-plus years from 1926 to 2004. (Courtesy of Ibbotson Associates)

Risk and Volatility

Of course, these long-term results, basking as they
are in the light of 20/20 hindsight, aren't the whole
story. Owning a company's stock is much riskier
than holding either U.S. government bonds or
cash. For one thing, stock prices and dividends
aren't guaranteed. They're bound to reflect the ups
and downs of the corporation's business.

For another, the ups and downs of both individual
stocks and the stock market as a whole can be
gut-wrenching. Consider the technology-heavy
NASDAQ stock exchange. It reached a high value
of 5,048 in March 2000. Roughly five years later, at
the end of March 2005, it stood at 1,999—just
more than a 60 percent drop. Decades from now,
historians may come to view this as a normal fluctuation, or even part of a long-term upward trend.
Right now, though, it looks like a pretty stunning
reversal of fortune.

Without a crystal ball, it's impossible to know for
sure what's coming next. But based on past history
and the basic differences between stocks, bonds,
and cash, it's likely that stocks will continue to
move up and down more steeply than either bonds
or cash.

One way to manage this volatility is by spreading
your money around. You can do that by investing
in different stocks, and by keeping some of your
money in bonds, cash, real estate (for example,
your home), and other assets, too. We discuss this
further in Chapter 5.

Ways to Invest

Just 20 years ago, investors basically had two choices: buy individual stocks through a broker at a firm such as Merrill Lynch or Smith Barney, or buy shares in a mutual fund run by professional managers. Now you have many more choices, and the ability to mix and match to suit yourself.

With a computer, an Internet connection, an online stock-trading account, and a little legwork, you can access everything necessary to research, buy, track, and sell stocks all by yourself. Just because you can, though, doesn't mean you should.

Do It Yourself

When you manage your own stock investments, you start with one big advantage: your services are free. That's a significant edge, because mutual-fund fees or brokers' commissions can suck up 1 percent or more of your investment dollars every year.

As long as you have an Internet connection, you can pay much less. You can trade online with a number of well-known companies for about $10 per trade. Of course you may (and probably should) opt to pay for extras such as research services, newsletters, and perhaps a few more books like this one. But you'll still be way ahead of the game on costs.

Which brings us to another consideration: no one cares about your money more than you do. That can be an advantage, if it means you'll work hard and choose carefully. Or it can be a disadvantage, if you procrastinate and make emotional decisions.

How can you figure out which type of investor you'll be? You can't know for sure until you actually do it. Still, there are some traits that many successful investors share:

- ◆ Are you the kind of person who enjoyed school? That's a plus, because stock picking requires two of the three "Rs"—reading and 'rithmetic.

- ◆ Are you an independent sort, not easily swayed by popular opinion? Chalk up another plus. Being a lemming in the stock market usually leads to disaster.

- ◆ Last, and perhaps most important, you need the time and energy to research stocks, keep track of your holdings, and make trades.

If this all sounds hard, it is. The sobering fact is that most professional money managers aren't able to beat the broad stock indexes consistently. And they work full time, with the best resources.

On the other hand, if you'd enjoy controlling how your money is invested, and if you've got the aptitude and the time it takes, you could be one of the legions of people who do very well by doing it themselves.

$ Market Speak

Want to know whether stocks in general are going up or down? Take a look at a stock market **index**, which measures the ups and downs of an entire group of stocks. If enough stocks are included, the movements of the index are a pretty good way to judge the movement of the market as a whole. In fact, when professionals talk about "the market," they're usually referring to the gain or loss in one of the big market indexes. The Standard & Poor's 500 Index is one of the best ways to judge the performance of the U.S. stock market. It includes the stocks of 500 of the largest American companies, representing about 80 percent of the dollar value of all U.S. stocks.

Get Help from an Advisor

Before the Internet brought trading capabilities to our desktops, full-service brokers were the most common way to invest in stocks. Nowadays, most firms call their brokers "financial advisors" and focus on giving advice, not making trades. Many offer a flat-fee arrangement (often 1 percent of your assets per year) and charge for trades on top of that. The costs of this sort of arrangement can really add up.

In theory, a good, experienced financial advisor who knows how to select stocks and structure a portfolio is worth the cost. In the real world, though, there just aren't a lot of them out there. What's more, the best financial advisors naturally prefer to work with the wealthiest clients. After all, 1 percent of $1,000,000 is a lot more than 1 percent of $100,000.

If it sounds like I'm not a big fan of traditional brokers, you're right. Unless you've got well over a million dollars to invest, you probably won't connect with someone whose advice is worth the price.

Use Mutual Funds

Mutual funds sell you shares in a portfolio of stocks, not just a single issue. They're a practical way for many small investors to pool their money. Mutual funds offer two main advantages. First, they let you own a broader range of stocks than you could on your own. Second, they can make professional management and administration more affordable by spreading the cost around.

The U.S. mutual fund in its current form came into being when Congress passed the Investment Company Act of 1940. But mutual funds really became popular about 20 years ago, when IRAs, 401(k)s, and other retirement accounts began to replace traditional pensions for many workers.

Today, roughly 8,000 mutual funds are available, giving you a way to invest in just about anything from technology to the Asian markets. Almost all of them fall into two broad categories: traditional and index.

Traditional mutual funds are run by a portfolio manager who selects stocks based on his or her investing style and expertise. Many funds of this kind have a specific focus—for example, large U.S. companies, energy firms, or foreign stocks. But all traditional funds aim to beat the performance of one or another index, whether an industry-specific index or a major market index, such as the Standard & Poor's 500.

Index funds, on the other hand, do exactly as their name suggests. They're designed to match an index, not beat it. The index in question can be anything from the S&P 500 to Japan's Nikkei, but the sole goal is always to keep the fund's return the same as its index.

You'll pay a fee to own either type of mutual fund. Typically, annual fees run between .5 and 2 percent for a managed fund. Index funds usually carry lower fees, because you're not paying for an expert's savvy. The largest of these, the Vanguard 500 Index Fund, charges a paltry $18 for a $10,000 investment.

> **Red Flags**
>
> You can't control the markets, but you can control the price you pay to be in them. The average management fees for a U.S. equity mutual fund add up to about 1.5 percent of your money every year. Full-service brokers can charge 1 percent of assets annually to manage your money. Even the fees for online trading services, with extras such as research, can add up over time. Expenses eat away at your returns year after year. So it's important to do a little shopping around to keep overhead on a permanent diet. We look into this subject in more detail in Chapter 4.

Mix and Match

Why choose between mutual funds and individual stocks when you can reduce your risks (and possibly actually increase returns) by using both?

We discuss this idea further in Chapter 5, but basically, I'd strongly advise just about everyone to consider putting at least some money into mutual funds to gain exposure to the broad markets. I'd also advise most people to invest in assets other than stocks. This includes negotiable securities such as bonds and tangible assets such as a home.

This way, the ups and downs of individual stocks can't make or break your finances. You can always stake more on your stock selections as you gain experience and confidence.

Market Myths Versus Reality

Remember the "new economy" blather that justi-
fied ultra-high stock prices for companies without
profits or significant revenues in the late 1990s?
How about the real estate mania in some regions of
the country, still flourishing as this book goes to
press? It seems that some clever investors have
decided that stocks are too risky, but house prices
will always go up!

This is a good spot to debunk these kinds of myths,
the type that fuel short-term, irrational thinking.
Instead, I'll focus on underlying truths you can rely
on for the long term.

**Myth: If everyone is doing something, it must
be right.**

Reality: It pays to think for yourself. The surest
way to be wrong is to follow the crowd instead of
asking simple questions based on your own ideas
and research.

**Myth: Only professionals can consistently find
good stock investments.**

**Reality: You can be a successful stock picker on
your own.** The average investor today has access to
more than enough information and trading resources to create and manage a stock portfolio. What
you make of this seeming wealth of information
depends mainly on your hard work and judgment—
just as it does for the pros.

Myth: Investing in stocks is extremely risky. You could lose everything.

Reality: You can limit your risks. For example, you can do your homework, make a financial plan, and avoid putting all your eggs in one basket by investing in different types of stocks, as well as in instruments besides stocks.

Myth: You can make a fortune by picking a winner.

Reality: Making money in stocks takes time and hard work. Thinking you'll pick a big winner and can neglect everything else is like thinking you'll win the lottery with a single ticket. You *could* manage to be both dumb and lucky, but the odds are hugely against it. Careful research, diligent tracking, patience, and strict control of risk aren't glamorous or exciting, but they're what it takes to be a successful long-term investor.

Taking Stock of Your Goals

Are you 25 or 55? Married with kids and a mortgage, or footloose and fancy-free? Planning for next year, or for the next generation? To a surprisingly large degree, your success as an investor will hinge on matching financial decisions to your wants and needs in life.

What Are You Investing For?

If you've got money you'll need to get at within the next year or two—or even within the next five years—stocks may not be your best bet. Whether you're planning to buy a home or car, or write a tuition check for your daughter's sophomore year in college, you want that money to be there, and to be largely intact. Think how frustrated you'd be if you were forced to sell stock in a good company at the depths of a market slump!

On the other hand, if you're investing for a retirement that's still decades away, you've got time to wait out a market decline. As long as you still think a stock you've chosen will show a profit in the long run, you've got the flexibility to stay invested.

In general, your stock money should be your patient money. Even if you *do* decide to put some money you may need in a year or so into stocks, be sure to choose stable, dividend-paying stocks and avoid more-volatile, faster-growing companies.

What Kind of an Investor Are You?

Some people can sleep soundly no matter what the market is doing, whereas others can find themselves counting losses or gains instead of sheep, deep into the night.

The key is to know yourself—in particular, to know your attitudes toward money and investing. It won't do any good to make bold stock picks if you'll bail out at the first hint of trouble. Nor will you be likely to prosper if you invest carefully, but manage neglectfully.

To quote Benjamin Graham, author of the 1934 investing classic *Security Analysis*, "The investor's chief problem—and even his worst enemy—is likely to be himself."

Think about investment decisions you've made in the past, both good and bad. These can include major purchases, apartment leases, and other big financial commitments. Be honest with yourself about how well you handled these, and how you'll likely handle similar tough decisions in the future. Then think about how to set up a stock portfolio you're sure you can live with.

The Secret of Success

People have made fortunes in the stock market in a number of ways: ferreting out unloved and undervalued businesses, getting the jump on advances in business or technology, finding new leaders in established fields, patiently staying the course with well-run market leaders—and in lots of other ways, too.

So what's the real secret of success? As you may have guessed from the variety of examples in this chapter, there is no one secret. I'm a firm believer that how well you do in the market depends not on gimmicks or formulas, but on how well you do as a researcher, a thinker, a manager, a planner.

So far I've asked you to think about what you're investing for, why you're investing, and what kind of investor you are. In the next chapter, we look at *where* you'll be investing. You guessed it—it's time to look at the markets!

The Least You Need to Know

- Investors need to spend ample time on research and analysis before actually buying stocks.

- Historically, stocks have been both more risky and more profitable when compared to bonds or cash.

- Stocks can make you money in two ways: through increases in share price and through dividend payments.

- There's no surefire recipe for success—but following the crowd is a surefire recipe for failure.

- Your stage of life, immediate financial needs, and tolerance for risk should determine how much you can put into stocks versus how much you put into other types of assets, such as bonds or a home.

2

Fasten Your Seatbelt

In This Chapter

- Why markets move
- Tracking the indexes
- Highs and lows in history
- Learning from the past

There was no outbreak of war, no government upheaval, no business scandal. Yet on October 19, 1987, the Dow Jones Industrial Average went down as if something disastrous had happened. By the end of the day, the Dow had plummeted 22.6 percent, its largest single-day percentage drop in modern market history. Broader markets were hit just about as hard, leaving stunned investors with staggering losses at the closing bell.

But was it really such a catastrophe? Looking back years later, we can see that it took just 16 months for the Dow to regain all the losses of October 19—and just 8 months for it to rebound to a loss of less than 5 percent. We can also see that the history of the markets is filled with dramatic ups and downs. From that perspective, that day looks less like a disaster and more like an extreme example of business as usual.

If you are going to invest in stocks, you need to know that you're not seeing a once-in-a-lifetime event every time a stock—or an index—shoots up or down. In this chapter, you'll learn why *volatility* really is business as usual, and what you can learn from past peaks and valleys.

> **($) Market Speak**
>
> When we're talking about individual stocks or stock markets, **volatility** refers to increases or declines in value. Stocks have historically been more volatile than other investments—such as bonds or cash—meaning prices move around more. It makes sense. Unlike bonds or cash, stocks don't come with a guarantee of repayment with interest. They're worth whatever investors will pay when you want to sell.

Why Markets Move

One way to think of stock markets is as polling places, where investors gather to size up current profits, future growth potential, possible risks, etc., and set the price at which they're willing to buy or sell a stock. In essence, the markets hold a never-ending election on each stock, with investors casting their votes by buying or selling.

According to this theory, prices of stocks change from day to day, or even from minute to minute, as new information becomes available and investors act accordingly. For example, when Wal-Mart sold less merchandise than expected during the 2004 holiday season, it put future sales forecasts and profits in doubt. As a result, investors collectively adjusted the price of Wal-Mart's stock downward by about 6 percent over two days of trading.

Fact Versus Fantasy

Sometimes it's not so much the facts that change but how investors feel about them. For example, online retailer Amazon.com saw its stock rise from $1.50 a share when it was first offered in 1997 to $106.69 (adjusted for *stock splits*) in December 1999, at the height of the Internet bubble. The price plunged from that peak all the way down to $5.97 in September 2001 following the September 11 terrorist attacks on the World Trade Center and the bursting of the Internet stock bubble, only to rebound again to $33.09 as of June 30, 2005 (see the figure that follows).

During all these ups and downs, Amazon's stated goal was always to build a profitable online retailing business. A rational investor, who focused on how Amazon was doing against that goal, probably wouldn't have bought the stock at the height of its popularity in 1999. Despite rapid growth, the company was losing money, to the tune of $882 million by the end of that year. And it was valued at a price that couldn't be justified by any realistic projection of continued growth. (We'll talk more about valuation in Chapter 8.)

The Bottom Line

Stock splits refer to the division of company shares. Two-for-one, three-for-one, and three-for-two splits are all relatively common. If you own 100 shares of a stock selling for $50, and it splits 2-1, you'll end up owning 200 shares of a stock selling for $25 instead. Note that splits have no effect on overall share value. When we compare share prices for companies over long periods, we simply adjust the share price to factor in whatever splits occurred.

If it doesn't change the value, why do companies split their shares at all? It's all psychological. Keeping prices down can make shares seem easier to afford to small investors, or even create the illusion of getting something for nothing. By the same principle, reverse splits—in which a company gives investors fewer, more-expensive shares—are sometimes used to make an embarrassingly low stock price appear higher.

On the other hand, that same rational investor might have found Amazon considerably more attractive by late 2001, when the company was still growing, still expanding its offerings, still focused on a growing consumer segment—and much more reasonably priced. Yet that's when most people were selling.

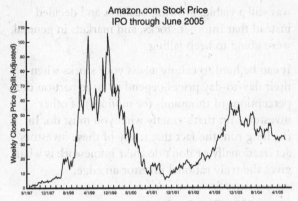

Amazon's stock price took a wild ride from its initial public offering in 1997 through June of 2005.

Ignoring the Crowd

We always know what has happened in the past, but we can only make educated guesses about what will happen in the future. As highly successful mutual-fund manager John Neff, of The Vanguard Group, puts it, "Most investors are great at extending straight lines."

As our Amazon.com example shows, investors in 2001 knew that Internet stocks in general, and Amazon in particular, had been grossly overvalued and had dramatically fallen in value. But they could only guess about what was next.

Most people did the natural thing and assumed the future was going to be similar to the present. In other words, they overlooked the fact that Amazon was still a viable, growing business and decided instead that Internet stocks, and markets in general, were going to keep falling.

It can be hard to calmly assess your stocks when their day-to-day prices depend in large part on the perceptions of thousands (or millions) of other investors. Yet that's exactly what you must do. In the long run, the fact that many of these investors act irrationally or don't do their homework is what gives the truly rational investor an edge.

How We Track the Markets

Before we discuss market volatility any further, let's take a brief but essential detour and review some of the most frequently used market measuring sticks.

It would be overwhelmingly complex and confusing to literally track every stock. Instead, professional money managers, investors, journalists, and everyone else rely on indexes of selected stocks to represent the broader market.

The Dow

Launched in 1896 by Charles Dow (who also founded the *Wall Street Journal*), the Dow Jones Industrial Average broke new ground in American stock market history by using a selected group of stocks to measure the direction of the markets as a whole.

Dow and his colleagues continued adding stocks to the index until it reached the current total of 30 in 1928. Since then, each time a stock has been added to the Dow, one has been removed. According to Dow Jones literature, "A stock typically is added only if it has an excellent reputation, demonstrates sustained growth [and] is of interest to a large number of investors."

Under these vague guidelines, the Dow today betrays its roots in the era of industrial America, with technology and service companies underrepresented. Coca-Cola and General Motors are in, Cisco and eBay aren't. Even mighty Microsoft didn't make it into the Dow until 1999.

So why is the Dow still so widely cited? For one thing, it remains a reasonably accurate snapshot of how large American companies are doing. But its longevity and status as the first modern stock index are probably the main reasons—one more example of how perception can shape reality in the markets.

The Standard & Poor's 500

The S&P index has a long history, too. It launched in 1923 with 223 stocks and reached the current 500 in 1957. With more stocks than the Dow, the S&P includes all major industries and is regularly updated to mirror changes in the overall markets. In short, it's a more balanced and representative sample of the U.S. stock market as a whole.

The largest companies in the U.S. markets are virtually all in the S&P 500. In fact, the stocks it includes make up about 80 percent of the value of the U.S. markets. Because it is big and broad, the S&P is the basis for much professional analysis of the markets.

The NASDAQ

Unlike the Dow and the S&P, the NASDAQ Composite is made up of all the stocks listed on a single exchange. Founded in 1971, the NASDAQ was the first stock market to be entirely computerized—hence its name: the National Association of Security Dealers Automated Quotations.

Its electronic approach, combined with lower fees and easier standards for listing, attracted fledgling technology companies. In the 1990s, many of those firms grew up fast. NASDAQ–listed newcomers such as Microsoft, Apple, Cisco, Intel, and eBay propelled the index from an upstart to a power player, and the NASDAQ's explosive growth was followed by legions of technology *bulls*.

Since then, the NASDAQ's value has declined, along with that of many of the technology stocks listed on it. But despite those negative perceptions, the NASDAQ remains a reasonable indicator for American technology stocks.

> **$ Market Speak**
>
> Bull markets are periods when stocks are going up. The phrase derives from the German "to roar." **Bear markets** are periods when markets are going down. The term *bear market* is thought to derive from the proverb "to sell the bear's skin before one has caught the bear," or what we now call short-selling—that is, hoping to profit from a decline in a stock price. The idea is to sell shares one doesn't own now to be delivered later, by which time we're hoping that the price will have fallen.). There's no single definition of how long or deep a rise or fall must be to qualify as a bull or bear market. But a change of plus or minus 20 percent or more, lasting at least 2 months, is a reasonable standard.

What About Foreign Markets?

Sure, the United States is the 800-pound gorilla of the world economy. But the European Union, Japan, China, India, and other areas aren't exactly 98-pound weaklings. And the very size of the U.S. economy means that the rest of the world is less developed by comparison, leaving room for greater future growth.

You can benefit from at least some of that growth by owning stock in U.S. corporations. For example, roughly 70 percent of Coca-Cola's revenue and operating income in 2004 came from countries outside North America. In Chapter 7, you'll learn how to find detailed financial information like this. Obviously, it's essential to making informed decisions.

But you can also expand your investing horizons to include companies listed on foreign stock exchanges. Many foreign companies make it easy, by letting you buy and sell their stocks in dollars on U.S. markets through *American Depository Receipts.*

> **⑤ Market Speak**
>
> **American Depository Receipts** were created more than 75 years ago as a way of buying and selling foreign stocks in U.S. markets. Banks create ADRs by buying a block of foreign stock and reissuing it for sale. The bank handles all the foreign currency conversion, so the stock trades in dollars, usually with the letters ADR following the company name. ADRs are usually priced very close to the shares of the stock in its home market, though there can be differences because markets operate in separate time zones. For instance, because the Tokyo market closes in the wee small hours of the New York morning, an ADR on a Japanese stock and its local share never trade at the same time.

When you invest in foreign stocks you have to consider more than just the company and industry you are buying—you also have to factor in currency exchange. If a company's home currency rises or falls against the dollar, it usually won't outweigh business realities, but it can make a big difference in your results. Political risk is another factor. Coups, wars, and other events can stop a company in its tracks. These two factors aren't a big worry for stocks in countries such as Germany or Japan. But for less-developed nations, the combination may simply be too much for individual investors to manage, and mutual funds may be a more realistic choice.

Translating the Foreign Indexes

Perhaps the best-known international index is the MSCI EAFE (Morgan Stanley Capital International Europe, Australasia, and Far East Index), known to traders as "ee-fuh" or "ee-fee." As the name suggests, it includes large companies from much of the world.

If non–U.S. economies continue to grow faster than ours, we can expect to read more about country-specific indexes, too. The indexes for the markets in London (FTSE), France (CAC), Germany (DAX), and Japan (Nikkei) are already widely published. In the future, we may find ourselves following indexes tracking the stock markets of China, India, Brazil, or other emerging countries, too.

Highs and Lows in History

From the Dutch tulip mania in the early 1600s to America's Great Depression of the 1930s, the history of investing is filled with booms and busts. If records existed for the earliest known markets, held at the Forum in ancient Rome, I think we'd probably find similar volatility back then, too.

The lessons of the past can help you invest in the future. In the interest of relevance, I'll skip ancient history, and focus on three more recent markets: the '70s, '80s, and '90s.

The Sluggish '70s

The postwar prosperity of the 1950s and 1960s had built confidence among many investors that the U.S. economy was an engine of constant growth. By the early 1970s, a group of large corporations known as the Nifty Fifty, which included General Electric, Coca-Cola, Xerox, and Avon, had been anointed by brokers as cornucopias of growth.

Undeniably, these large companies had grown steadily, boosted by a soaring American economy and low interest rates. Most had also been regularly increasing dividends. And because they were big companies with large amounts of stock in the market, share prices had risen relatively gradually.

But that changed as investors rushed in. Professor and author Jeremy Siegel of the Wharton Business School has calculated that the Nifty Fifty stocks

reached a peak in 1972, with an average *price/
earnings (P/E) ratio* of 41.9, more than twice the
18.9 average P/E of the S&P 500 stocks.

> **($)** **Market Speak**
>
> **Price/earnings ratio,** or P/E for
> short, is the ratio of a company's
> earnings to the price of a share of stock.
> Typically earnings are based on the last
> four full quarters. For example, if a com-
> pany earned $5 per share profits over the
> previous year and shares were selling for
> $100, the P/E would be $100 divided
> by $5, or 20. Rapidly growing compa-
> nies often have higher P/E ratios than
> more-established businesses, because
> investors are factoring future growth into
> the price. In fact, you'll sometimes see a
> leading or projected P/E ratio for a com-
> pany, based on estimates of future earn-
> ings rather than past results.

Eventually, investors were bound to realize that
favorable economic and political conditions weren't
going to propel earnings on an uninterrupted jour-
ney to new heights. The Arab oil embargo of
1973–74 led to a world economic slowdown and
triggered a sharp drop in profits at many companies. The Watergate scandal in Washington, D.C.,
added political uncertainty to the mix, and stock
prices were cut nearly in half by 1974.

Once-burned, twice-cautious investors remained wary of stocks for most of the remainder of the decade. Following a rally in 1975, the market more or less stood still compared to inflation from 1976 through 1982.

Meanwhile, General Electric, IBM, and many other well-run companies kept right on making profits, paying dividends, and even finding ways to grow during those five years. But most investors didn't care. They voted not to buy shares at reasonable prices, based on past bad experiences when they bought at unreasonable prices.

> ◢ **Red Flags**
>
> Safety in numbers can be an expensive illusion. In the early 1970s, investors flocked to Polaroid, attracted by its unique technology, new products, and sales of high-profit film packs. No one wanted to miss out, and demand drove the price to a peak of $149 per share in 1972. Investors looking for true safety in numbers would have been better served by noting Polaroid's P/E ratio: it got as high as 95 in 1972. In other words, investors were paying $95 for every $1 of actual earnings. No amount of future growth could justify that price, and by December 1974, Polaroid shares had fallen to about $18.

The Soaring '80s

Hindsight is always 20/20, and it seems obvious
now that stocks were primed to rise in the 1980s.
At the time, though, President Jimmy Carter was
lamenting America's malaise and investors wanted
safer places to stash their cash. High inflation made
15 percent interest rates available on federally
insured bank CDs, giving people little incentive to
look elsewhere.

But inflation also meant that valuations for many
stocks had quietly gone way down, even as prices
remained fairly stable. From an average P/E ratio
of about 19 on December 31, 1972, the S&P 500
stocks were down almost 50 percent, to an average
P/E of less than 9 on December 31, 1979.

At the same time, oil price deregulation, interest
rates, airline fares, and telephone charges helped
spark business activity. Inflation was reined in, with
Federal Reserve Board chairman Paul Volcker lead-
ing the fight. And mergers and acquisitions boomed
as alert businesspeople snapped up undervalued
companies.

Remember the market crash of October 19, 1987?
It came in the thick of the '80s bull run, caused
perhaps by a series of events—including a short-
term rise in interest rates, proposed legislation that
would have made takeovers much less attractive,
and a large trade deficit. All of these events may
have reminded investors that stocks were priced for
problem-free economic and political conditions
(remember 1973–74 and the Nifty Fifty?). And as

often happens in downturns, something new and unexpected occurred—in this case, the effect of computerized trading programs that triggered a wave of selling in response to market declines.

But memories of the past didn't coincide with present economic realities, and stock prices quickly recovered. That didn't mean there weren't big losers. Investors who followed the crowd and sold stocks in the downturn missed out not only on the gains of the previous years, but on subsequent gains.

The Bottom Line

World events and economic conditions change, but some of the basic ways of measuring an individual company's value are remarkably stable. At the start of 1989, Intel began a 5-year run in which it returned an average of 39 percent a year. Investors wondering whether to buy or sell throughout this time could have taken a cue from the company's price/earnings ratio, which barely budged, averaging a bit over 12 even as the stock's price regularly hit new highs. The relatively stable P/E provided evidence that Intel's growing stock price was backed by earnings that were growing just as fast.

The Bubbling '90s

Low interest rates and solid economic growth gave investors reason to expect a continuation of the 1980s bull market. But there were changes below the surface—price/earnings ratios were now higher for the Dow and S&P 500, and many of the most-undervalued companies had already been acquired or had risen in price.

Most important, lots of new investors were entering the markets. They were drawn by self-directed retirement accounts such as IRAs and 401(k)s and new, easier ways to buy and sell stocks in the form of discount brokerages. Increased media coverage of the booming markets also played a role. In any event, lots of new money was flowing into stocks, with not enough places to go.

When a hot new thing appeared, it was almost inevitable there'd be a rush to get in. In the late 1990s, that hot new thing was the Internet. Jeff Bezos, founder and CEO of Amazon.com, was fond of saying "It's day one for the Internet." And who wouldn't want to get in at the start of something big?

Suddenly, profits mattered less than concepts. New companies with no profits and no obvious prospects of making any not only sold stock, they had investors fighting to buy. One company that hosted online chat and message boards, theglobe.com, went to market at $9 a share in 1998, and ended its first day at $63.50—up more than ten-fold.

You probably know the rest. Internet and technology stocks raised the NASDAQ index to record highs before the air went out of the bubble with a rush in late 2000. Less than 3 years later, it was down more than 70 percent, and many of the Internet stocks that had led the run-up weren't just down, they were out of business altogether.

History's Lessons

Even the most successful stock pickers are far from infallible. There are too many intangibles. Consider, for example, the management of Hasbro. Who would have bought stock in a stodgy, family-run toy company back in 1981? If you'd only known that Hasbro was about to be revitalized by a new CEO who'd reignite its flagship G.I. Joe line of action figures for boys and launch a mega-hit with My Little Pony figures for girls, you could have increased your investment more than 50-fold over the next decade.

Or take financial malfeasance. It's hard enough to understand how a company makes money and what its assets are worth when management is honest. When they are not, it can be virtually impossible. Fraud was a major reason prudent investors shunned stocks in the early part of the century. And although government regulation, uniform accounting standards, and public scrutiny have improved things, human nature ensures that they will never be perfect.

Just ask anyone who saw his shares in Enron become worthless when the financial deceptions practiced by the company's top management were exposed.

In other words, the first lesson of history is to do your homework. No one can foresee the future, but anyone can see present-day facts if he or she looks hard enough. Knowing all you can about a company's management, finances, and lines of business is the best way to find opportunities—and avoid mistakes.

Any parent could have seen that Hasbro's toys were popular and followed up with some research on the business behind them. And any investor who couldn't understand how Enron's business worked could have avoided investing in the company's stock. I know I did (Theresa), for precisely that reason.

Red Flags

Whenever someone supports a high stock price with the argument that "it's different this time," watch out! The new economy rhetoric of the Internet bubble is just the latest example of hope trumping hard economic realities. When financial information and tangible business prospects don't support a stock's market valuation, history suggests something's got to give. Sticking to stocks whose value you can understand will help ensure you're not the one doing the giving.

Recent History

Volatility doesn't always mean going to extremes. We've been focusing on some of the highest highs and lowest lows, but in a more typical year, market moves will be more muted.

Let's look at 2004, which was a pretty average year by historical standards. Overall, the S&P 500 stocks were up an average of 11 percent. And there were only about 35 stocks that gained or lost more than 50 percent. So home runs and strikeouts were both pretty rare.

But average performance wasn't the norm, either. Only about 80 stocks actually earned 11 percent (give or take a tenth or a percent or two) in 2004. That left about two thirds of the stocks in a broad band around the average, with returns of -15 percent on the low end and +35 percent on the high.

It's a Good Time to Invest When ...

… stocks are at low price/earnings ratios compared to historic averages. Under these conditions, you're more likely to have room to turn a profit.

So part of doing your homework should be comparing past and present price earnings for individual stocks and the market as a whole. When you find a good business trading at a low price relative to its earnings, there could be room for the stock to rise.

In broader terms, think about the economy. It's the biggest single determinant of long-term returns from the stock market. Is the gross domestic product (the value of all goods and services produced in the United States) growing strongly? Are interest rates low? Do government tax and regulatory policies favor business? What about other factors, such as the prices of raw materials? Political instability or war?

It's easy to write nice, neat little stories to sum up past eras. Try writing a story for the present, instead. And be sure to ask yourself some tough questions while you're at it. How will your idea fare in different economic circumstances? Could the company still do okay even if you're wrong? And don't forget to evaluate your results in context. When the markets are down, breaking even can count as victory.

It's a Bad Time to Invest When ...

... your neighbors are talking about a stock, it's on the front page of the newspaper, and it's featured on TV. Everyone knows it's *the* thing to buy, or in some cases sell—right? Wrong!

Investor sentiment is a very reliable *contrary* indicator of market trends. In the late 1990s, everyone was plunging into technology stocks regardless of price. In the late 1970s, no one wanted undervalued stocks at any price.

If you learn one thing from this book, it should be to listen to facts and points of view that make clear, rational sense. And ignore the clamor of the crowd, however loud it may sometimes become.

The Least You Need to Know

- ◆ Staying focused on business information can help you respond rationally to changing stock values.

- ◆ Indexes are the most common way to keep track of what markets are doing.

- ◆ A stock's price/earnings ratio, or P/E for short, is the ratio of a company's earnings to the price of its shares.

- ◆ Specific business information and general economic conditions are better long-term investing guidelines than popular opinion.

Chapter 3

Investment Basics

In This Chapter

- How stocks and markets work
- What are stocks worth?
- Stock-picking styles
- How mutual funds work

Suppose you wake up tomorrow with a great idea for a business. You've got everything figured out, but you don't have enough money to get started by yourself. So you go to 3 of your friends and offer to sell them each 25 percent of your business, keeping 25 percent ownership for yourself.

That's the simple idea behind all stocks—companies get money, investors get a piece of the business.

Now suppose it's a year later, and your friend Fran wants to sell her share. By this time, your business is up and running. It's made some sales and has at least the prospect of profits to come. Fran sets her asking price based on this information. But she may find that buyers offer less—or more—based on their own ideas and information.

That's the simple idea behind the stock markets: investors buy and sell shares in companies for what they think they're worth.

Although the basic ideas are simple, the mechanics aren't. Before you involve yourself and your money, it's a good idea to understand how stocks and markets work in the real world.

Market Mechanics

First of all, the small start-up company we just described would be highly unlikely to sell stock on any market. After all, who would want to invest without knowing you and hearing your idea first-hand? That's why new companies generally get their first "seed" money from personal savings, family, friends, a loan, or sometimes from investors who specialize in funding start-ups.

After a company gets going, it can offer stock in the business to outsiders. At that point, people can look at the financial and business results and decide whether they want in, and at what price.

One choice available to companies is limiting stock sales to a few hand-picked investors. This is called a "private placement." Advantages for a firm's owners can include maintaining control of the business and avoiding the stricter accounting and reporting requirements that come with listing a stock for sale to the general public.

However, it's often not possible to find a small group of investors willing to agree to the terms—or come up with the amounts—a company wants. For huge corporations such as IBM or Kimberly-Clark, it's almost impossible. That's why most companies of any size opt to sell stock to the general public.

Issuing Shares

Before a company can make a public offering of stock, the owners need to define what rights shares will give investors. For example:

♦ What percentage of the company is each share worth?

♦ Will shares pay a dividend?

♦ Are shareholders allowed to vote for the board of directors or on important company policies?

Management must register this information, along with financial information about the company, with the Securities and Exchange Commission, or SEC. The SEC is the federal agency that regulates the financial industry, and it requires all publicly traded companies to file financial reports and other documents regularly, typically every three months.

Types of Shares

Not all shares of stock are created equal. When we talk about stocks, we usually mean *common stock*, the basic unit of corporate ownership, which usually includes the right to elect the board of directors and vote on other key policies.

But some companies also issue nonvoting common stock, or common stock with limited voting rights. Usually the reason is to protect control of a family or individual, and the voting shares often don't trade publicly at all.

Then there's *preferred stock*, which offers a fixed dividend that's paid before common stock–holders get a cent. Preferred stock offers a nice, secure income stream, similar to a bond. So the underlying ability of the company to make its payments is your main concern. Because the dividend you get is locked in, you can't make more, no matter how well the business does.

Some companies also issue *convertible securities*. These usually work like preferred stock, paying locked-in dividends, or like a bond, paying guaranteed interest, but with a provision that allows them to be turned into shares of common stock in the future.

Getting Listed

The first time a company sells shares is called an initial public offering, or IPO. When a company that has already issued stock decides to sell more shares, it's called a secondary offering.

In either case, a company usually works with an investment bank to set a price and line up large buyers (such as mutual funds and brokerage houses). After all, this is its big chance to raise money. After the shares are sold, any future profits go to the investors who own them.

($) Market Speak

Why are **convertible securities** often called "all-weather vehicles"? Because they provide both protection against a drop in the stock price and an opportunity to profit from any gains. If the price rises, you'll start thinking about converting your shares into common stock. (Each convertible security can eventually be exchanged into a specified number of shares.) But if the price falls, you'll be glad for the income you'll receive, since convertibles pay either interest or a fixed dividend.

A free lunch? Unfortunately not. Peace of mind always has a cost. In this case, when you buy a convertible, you'll pay a hefty premium over the value of the shares you will ultimately own. And the companies that issue convertibles tend to be riskier than most. That means careful research is required.

As part of planning its IPO, the company chooses the stock market on which its shares will be listed for sale. Although the SEC regulates the company, the exchanges often impose additional listing requirements—including size, financial resources, and reporting standards.

Conflicts of Interest

The very same investment banks that earn massive fees helping companies take stock to market often have brokerage arms that rate those very same stocks. The potential conflict of interest is obvious.

One particularly spectacular example from the recent past involved Jack Grubman, a prominent analyst at Salomon Smith Barney. Grubman continually raised his price forecasts for Global Crossing, WorldCom, and other telecommunications stocks in the late 1990s and early 2000s.

At the same time, Grubman and his firm had lucrative business dealings with many of the same firms he covered. "What used to be a conflict is now a synergy," Grubman boasted to *BusinessWeek* in May 2000. "Objective? The other word for it is uninformed."

When the telecom stocks he pushed crashed and burned (including multi-billion-dollar bankruptcies for Global Crossing and WorldCom), the legions of investors who followed his advice were left holding the bag.

Recently, both regulators and the major investment firms have taken steps to address blatant conflicts like this one. But it's still important to remember that information is only as good as its source, so be sure to read the fine print.

Browsing the Markets

Larger, more-established firms generally list on the larger and more established stock exchanges—such as the New York Stock Exchange (NYSE), or the London Stock Exchange, which traces its origins to seventeenth-century coffeehouses that were gathering places for speculators.

There are lots of choices. In addition to the NYSE, the United States has the NASDAQ, where many technology firms are listed. There are also smaller exchanges, including the American Stock Exchange (AMEX) and regional exchanges in Boston, Chicago, Philadelphia, and San Francisco. And virtually every country of any size has at least one stock exchange.

Some companies don't list on any exchange. These unlisted stocks are bought and sold through a network of over-the-counter dealers. In general, they're the smallest and riskiest companies. The term *penny stocks* is sometimes used to describe them.

 The Bottom Line

When you buy stock, you generally don't get a document, the way you do when you buy a house or a car. Each country does have an organization that keeps track, though. In the United States, it's the Depository Trust Company, part of the Federal Reserve System, that digitally records share ownership.

What Does a Market Look Like?

A stock market can a physical place. The New York Stock Exchange (NYSE) has a famous building on Wall Street. When you buy or sell shares in a company traded on the NYSE, your order is sent to a "floor broker." The floor broker walks over to a "specialist," someone who handles trading for your stock.

The specialist knows how the stock is priced, and can quickly find someone to take the other side of your trade—to buy if you are selling, to sell if you're buying. When the price is agreed on, the specialist tells the floor broker, who then confirms the trade.

All stock markets used to work this way, but now most conduct business either partially or entirely electronically. Even the NYSE processes small stock orders electronically. And on the NASDAQ there are no floor brokers or specialists at all. Buyers and sellers contact each other directly using the market's software and trading systems.

Computerized systems matching buyers and sellers around the world are a topic of endless analysis within the financial industry. Making sure pricing and access are fair is very important to big brokerages and money managers, and there's heated competition to make execution of trades ever more efficient.

Increasingly, computerized trading is blurring the borders between markets as it transforms their central function from physical places to trade stocks into systems with set rules and regulations.

How Much Does the Market Matter?

The market on which a company is listed doesn't matter much to you as an investor. But it does matter that a stock be listed on an established, well-regulated market.

It probably doesn't matter if a Midwestern industrial firm happens to be listed on the Chicago Stock Exchange rather than the NYSE. But it could matter a lot if it's unlisted, or if you're buying a foreign stock listed on an exchange you've never heard of.

Companies that trade on established exchanges are subject to wider scrutiny, must generally provide more information, and have more to lose if they misrepresent facts and finances. This is because you will be buying stock based in large part on the financial and business information the company provides.

What's more, established markets are designed to make sure stock prices reflect public buying and selling among a large number of people and financial institutions—not backroom dealings among a few cronies.

For these two reasons, you are strongly advised to stick to stocks traded on well-known and well-regulated markets. Chances are, though, your research will lead you toward these companies anyway.

How You Make Money

As mentioned in Chapter 1, there are only two ways to make money from stocks. The first is capital appreciation, selling your shares to someone else for a higher price than you bought them for. The second is dividend income, a piece of a company's earnings that's paid out to stockholders.

Capital Appreciation

Stocks don't have one value, they have several. The first and simplest is the price that shares are selling for at any given moment.

Then there's the longer-term, underlying value of the issuing corporation. If there are a million shares of a company, each share represents ownership of one millionth of the company. Shareholders essentially own a small piece of the company's financial assets, such as cash and investments; physical assets, such as real estate and equipment; intellectual assets, such as copyrights and patents; and business assets, such as contracts with customers. Those assets are offset by costs, including payroll, rent, materials, and utilities. They also include outstanding loans, bond payments, and other financial commitments.

Beyond that, investors may also weigh a stock's *future* value. As an example, following the bursting of the Internet bubble, some companies had *market caps* lower than the value of the cash they still had on hand from their IPOs! Investors knew these companies were going to spend that money on expenses and had no way of earning more, so they downgraded the future value of the stock accordingly. On the other hand, stock in a company with no profits and little money in the bank can still be valuable if the company has strong prospects for future business growth.

> **$ Market Speak**
>
> **Market capitalization,** a.k.a. **market cap,** is the value of all shares in a company. It's calculated by multiplying the number of shares times the current price. So a company with a million shares selling for $10 each would have a market cap of $10,000,000. One way to judge a stock's value is to calculate the market cap of the company behind it; it should match up favorably with the value of the actual business. Companies are also often described or grouped by cap size, roughly as follows:
>
> **Micro cap:** Less than $250 million
> **Small cap:** $250 million to $1 billion
> **Mid cap:** $1 billion to $10 billion
> **Large cap:** More than $10 billion

Dividend Income

Dividends are the second way you can make money from stocks. They're calculated per share and are usually paid quarterly, although companies sometimes make special distributions, too.

The amount paid is set (or declared, in marketspeak) by the company's board of directors. For example, if you own 100 shares of a company paying a quarterly dividend of 5 cents a share, you'll receive a check or electronic funds transfer for $5 every three months.

Many companies give you the option of using your dividends to buy more stock through dividend reinvestment plans, or DRIPs. If shares are selling for $50 each, your $5 dividend would let you add one tenth of a share to your account every quarter.

After you sign up, DRIPs reinvest for you automatically, so they're convenient. Most charge low fees or no fee at all. And some even give you a discount on the price of the shares. As long as you want to keep buying stock and don't need the cash, I recommend enrolling in DRIPs whenever you can.

Dividends Versus Capital Gains

Historically, dividends and capital gains have gone back and forth in relative importance. From the 1920s into the 1970s, dividend payments were prized as a source of income, with capital appreciation often seen as a secondary benefit.

The tables turned during the long bull market that stretched from 1982 through 2000. With the economy strong, many managements chose to reinvest earnings in their businesses rather than paying them out as dividends. For example, fast-growing technology firms such as Cisco Systems and Microsoft paid no dividends in their early years, but capital appreciation kept shareholders happy.

During this period, many companies also used earnings to buy back their own stock. This created value for shareholders by supporting the price of shares. But it had another important effect: it helped increase the value of stock options.

Stock Options and Taxes

Stock options have become a popular way to tie executive pay to the performance of the company. The thinking is that if the CEO benefits from rising share prices through stock options, he will be motivated to run the business in the best interests of shareholders. During the Internet boom of the late 1990s and early 2000, options became the incentive of choice for all levels of employees, who saw a chance to strike it rich as share prices rose.

> ⑤ **Market Speak**
>
> **Stock options** give employees, usually executives, the right to buy a certain number of shares at some time in the future at a preset price. Normally, an executive can't exercise these non-qualified or incentive options right away, but has to wait a year or more for them to vest. What happens then? Suppose your option agreement says that you're allowed to purchase 1,000 shares at $50. If the market price is currently $60, you can make a profit of $10,000 (minus trading costs) simply by buying your shares and immediately reselling them.

But for options to be valuable, share prices had to keep rising—dividends didn't count. This meant management had a vested interest in propping up prices with stock buybacks. And investors didn't complain about buybacks taking the place of dividends ... as long as share prices kept rising.

Taxes played a role, too. For one thing, people became increasingly aware that dividends were taxed twice: once as income to the company, and once as income to the shareholder they were paid to.

And whereas dividends were taxed as income every year, just like your salary, increases in share prices were taxed at a lower capital gains rate, and you only paid when you actually sold your shares. Obviously investors in higher income tax brackets had good reason to prefer capital gains to dividends.

The Tax Act of 2003 changed that, by placing a flat tax rate of 15 percent on dividends—the same as on capital gains. Meanwhile, shareholders have revolted against the hidden costs of stock options and are more likely to pay executives with grants of dividend-paying stock rather than grants of options. In other words, as of 2005, the pendulum is swinging back toward dividends.

How Mutual Funds Work

Although this book is about buying individual stocks, mutual funds are simply too important to leave out completely. Mutual funds provide one-stop shopping for investors. You can own shares in lots of companies by buying shares in just one mutual fund.

There are more than 8,000 mutual funds in the United States, and you can find one specializing in just about any industry, investment philosophy, or stock type you can name. Shares are valued by adding up the value of the stocks owned and subtracting expenses. The resulting sum is called net asset value (NAV).

To illustrate, assume you start your own (very small) mutual fund. You sell 100 shares each to your husband, your parents, and your in-laws, and hire Jo to manage the investments and Fred to audit the books. Jo buys 100 shares of Little Women Clothing Stores, now worth $51 a share, for a total of $5,100. To compute the net asset value, you take the value of the assets and deduct the $100 you owe Jo and Fred for their work, to arrive at $5,000. Net asset value is usually stated as an amount per share, so you divide by 500 (the number of shares you've issued to your nearest and dearest), for a net asset value of $10 per share.

I highly recommend including mutual funds in your investment portfolio, along with individual stocks. As you'll see in Chapter 5, they can help you avoid putting too much of your investment nest egg in any one basket.

Index Funds

An index fund is a mutual fund that buys shares to match a specific stock market index. So a Standard & Poor's 500 index fund doesn't try to beat its benchmark, but simply to match it.

The Vanguard Group offered the very first index fund in 1975, spurred by John Bogle, the company's founder. Bogle saw index funds as a way to drastically cut management fees, because running one required no research or expert analysis. Index funds require only administrative support to make sure they stay on target.

"I projected the costs of managing an index fund to be 0.3 percent per year in operating expenses and 0.2 percent a year in transaction costs," Bogle said in his book *Character Counts: the Creation and Building of the Vanguard Group* (McGraw-Hill, 2002). "Because fund annual costs at that time appeared to be about 2 percent, I concluded that an index fund should reasonably be expected to provide an annual *return* of +1.5 percent above a managed fund."

(S) Market Speak

Return or **total return** measures a stock's performance by combining all the ways investors earn money, including both capital appreciation and dividends or other cash distributions. For instance, a stock paying a 1 percent dividend that has gone up in price by 5 percent would provide a 6 percent total return. It's the measure most often used by professional investors to size up how a stock has done.

Besides being inexpensive to run, index funds are a
simple way to spread your money around among
different markets. Buy shares in a Russell 2000
Index fund and you'll own 2,000 U.S. small cap
companies. Buy shares in an EAFE Index fund and
you own larger companies in Europe and Asia.
With index funds, you always know exactly what
you're getting.

Exchange Traded Funds

Exchange traded funds, or ETFs, are index funds
you buy on an exchange rather than from a mutual-
fund company. To create an ETF, a bank or other
financial institution buys and manages a portfolio
of stocks to match a specific index, then sells shares
to investors.

The major advantage of ETFs over conventional
index funds is that they can be traded instantly at
any time during the day. Mutual funds, by contrast,
can be purchased or sold only when the net asset
value (NAV) is calculated, which is usually at the
end of the trading day.

On the other hand, brokers charge commissions for
buying and selling ETF shares. And there are ongoing fees, just as there are for index mutual funds.

Managed Funds

Managed funds depend on people to pick their
stocks. As noted, the fees for that guidance make
managed funds more expensive than index funds.

In return, they offer just one advantage: the wisdom of the people picking the stocks.

Because I was once one of those people, I'd like to be able to tell you we're worth it. But the truth is, only a few of us are.

Sure, Peter Lynch ran circles around the market indexes when he ran the Magellan Fund for Fidelity Investments from 1977 to 1990. And there are other well-run managed funds, too. Many have lowered expenses, too, and offer strong management at a good price. Unfortunately, most managed funds are simply so-so, and not worth the extra cost.

These days, it's hard to argue against the simplicity, focus, and low cost of index funds for at least some of your portfolio.

Closed-End Funds

Most mutual funds are open-ended, meaning shares are bought and sold by the mutual fund company every evening. But closed-end mutual funds sell shares only occasionally. In between, the shares trade on a stock market, just like any other corporation.

Generally, shares of closed-end funds sell for less than the total value of the stocks the fund owns (although they also occasionally can sell for more). This discount doesn't seem to make much sense, but the most widely accepted explanation is that it reflects investor doubts about how well fund management will do in the future.

Whatever the reason or reasons, you won't want to buy shares in a closed-end fund at full price when they're issued, because the price is likely to fall. When they're being traded on the market, though, discounts can make a closed-end fund a good value.

Both *Barron's* and the *Wall Street Journal* list closed-end funds each week, with the discount or premium for each compared with its net asset value.

The Least You Need to Know

- ◆ Markets don't have to be physical places anymore; computers are often used to match stock buyers and sellers.

- ◆ Stocks are valued by present market price, underlying business value, and future prospects.

- ◆ Stock investors earn money in two ways— dividends and capital appreciation—that go back and forth in relative importance.

- ◆ Mutual funds let you own many stocks through a single investment vehicle.

Chapter 4

Choosing a Broker

In This Chapter

♦ The high cost of advice
♦ Picking a reliable discount broker
♦ Setting up an account
♦ Understanding stock orders

Imagine if the stock market worked like a flea market. You could stroll around the exchange floor, browse the wares, haggle over prices—even set up a booth of your own to sell your slightly used shares of Intel or Toys 'R' Us to anyone who stopped by.

Obviously, that's not how things work. Whether it's the New York Stock Exchange or Hong Kong's, the Bourse in Paris, or the completely electronic network that makes up the NASDAQ, nowhere in the world can you trade stock shares as your own agent. Instead, you have to hire an intermediary, in the form of a brokerage firm.

Up until about 30 years ago, if you were going to buy stocks or bonds, you did it through a flannel-suited stockbroker—as mythic an American figure as the family doctor or used-car salesman. Stockbrokers all worked for clubby Wall Street firms, and the hefty commissions these firms charged were fixed by law; no discounts were possible or even imaginable. But starting in 1975, deregulation began to change all that.

Today, you've got more options for trading than ever. Should you opt for one of the full-service outfits, as in your father's day, or a discount firm with much cheaper commissions? Pay someone to do your research, or do it yourself? Buy or sell only after conferring with a personal advisor, or fill out a web page and click the Send button? And who in this jungle of clamoring services can you really trust?

Fortunately, it's not as hard as it might seem. Your most important choice will be between full-service and discount. This chapter leads you through the key factors to consider, after which you can do further research on your own. You'll learn about the basics of setting up an account and the different kinds of orders you can place for stocks.

Full-Service Versus Discount Brokers

Full-service firms include such well-known names as Merrill Lynch, Smith Barney, and UBS. They're generally very large and well-staffed; they typically have an investment banking division, a research division, and a sales division, where the stockbrokers work. Only they're not called stockbrokers anymore, but "financial advisors."

> ### Bulls & Bears
>
> Financial service companies want you to believe that you can't make financial decisions yourself so they can collect lucrative fees. Remember the words of Woody Allen: "A stockbroker is someone who invests other people's money until it is all gone."
> —Burton G. Malkiel, *The Random Walk Guide to Investing: Ten Rules for Financial Success* (W. W. Norton & Company, 2005)

Thirty years ago full-service firms made most of their profits on *commissions*, or per-trade fees, but deregulation drove them to seek additional ways of making money. Today, they're concentrating on capturing wealthy customers to whom they can offer prepackaged financial advice under the rubric of "wealth management."

When it comes to investing in stocks, full-service firms typically boast that they've got great research and superior recommendations. In the past, both the research and the recommendations have tended to be biased in favor of whatever companies the firm is promoting as an investment banker.

Full-service firms have done a lot to clean up their acts in this regard, but it's still an issue in the eyes of some critics.

Discounters, meanwhile, got their start with deregulation. The arrival of Internet trading in the 1990s gave them a further boost. Historically, they've emphasized a no-frills approach, with little in the way of research and recommendations.

The *premium discounters* such as Schwab and E*TRADE now offer at least some financial advice, depending on how much money you park with them. They may give you a free portfolio analysis via telephone consultation, or provide investment recommendations if you call their customer service department. Other discount firms, sometimes known as *deep discounters*, stick with the original philosophy of cheap trades and no advice.

> **(S) Market Speak**
>
> When is a discount brokerage not a discount brokerage? Some firms, such as Schwab and E*TRADE, have begun to offer more online tools and financial advice, even as their fees and commissions have inched upward. The financial magazine *SmartMoney* has taken to calling these upwardly mobile firms **premium discounters**. Taking the opposite tack are the **deep discounters**, who continue to offer skeleton-bare service and rock-bottom commissions to match.

Even with the plusher discounters, you could well talk to someone different every time you call with a question, and your main means of communication will be via an impersonal website. With a full-service firm, you get your own personal broker or financial advisor, who does her best to cultivate a relationship with you.

The High Cost of the Personal Touch

Just how much more expensive are the full-service firms when it comes to trading? Commissions can be hard to pin down, and they change often, but the general answer is: a lot.

Here's an example. *SmartMoney*, a savvy monthly financial magazine put out by the folks at the *Wall Street Journal*, does an annual broker survey. In their 2004 survey, they noted that it would have cost you $437 to buy 1,000 shares of a $20 stock through UBS, the priciest of the full-service brokers surveyed that year. Meanwhile, the same trade through a discount broker would have cost you $32.95 at a relatively plush discounter like Schwab, and even less at a bare-bones discounter, as little as $5 or $10.

Commissions do vary noticeably between full-service brokers. But regardless, opting for full-service rather than discount will dramatically increase your trading costs—a difference that could amount to tens of thousands of dollars over your investing lifetime.

Have Assets, Want Super-Broker

So far, the full-service firms sound like a bust. Their commissions are too high, their research has been biased, and their brokers are under pressure to sell you expensive extras you may not need, such as annuities or mediocre portfolio advice. What advantage could they possibly offer the dedicated investor?

Actually, there are a few—the first and foremost being that the big-name firms are home, here and there, to a handful of financial advisors who happen to be truly good stock pickers.

 The Bottom Line

If you *do* pick a full-service firm as your broker, you'll find you can use their research to your advantage without worrying much about bias. First, when reading an analyst's report, throw out the part mostly likely to be tainted—the recommendation to buy or sell. You'll be left with good basic info about the company. Next, do as Peter Lynch suggests, and turn your broker into your legman. Don't just ask him what he thinks about a stock; ask him to gather the recent earnings data, the P/E ratio relative to historic levels, the percentage of shares owned by institutional investors, and whatever else you're interested in. He'll be glad to do it when he sees you're serious.

Advisors of this quality tend to be more like independent contractors than employees. If they move from one firm to another, their satisfied customers usually move with them. This built-in client base gives them the luxury of ignoring pressure from the firm to sell bad advice or overpriced products.

There's a catch, of course, and it's a big one. These thoroughbreds usually work only with serious investors with large accounts. As mentioned in Chapter 1, if you've got $1 million or more to invest, that should be enough to get a super-broker to consider you as a client if he's got room. You *could* try and get his attention with less than that— say, a minimum of $250,000—but it's going to be a much tougher sell.

Assuming you have the big bucks, here's how I'd go about searching for one of these rare overachievers:

- Go to *SmartMoney* on the web, at www. smartmoney.com, and look up the magazine's most recent survey of full-service brokerages. Pick a few of the higher-rated firms to start with.

- Call the local offices of these firms and talk with the manager. Ask which brokers have the largest book of business. Then ask who specifically concentrates on stock-picking; you're not interested in someone who mainly works with local companies' 401(k) plans.

- When you have your list of broker names, call them up and arrange to interview them. Keep in mind they'll also be interviewing you. Do you have enough in assets? Are you serious about stocks? Brokers prefer clients who are clear about what they want and act consistently with stated intentions.

◆ Also check their regulatory record with the NASD (National Association of Securities Dealers); you can do this online at www.nasd.com, using their BrokerCheck feature.

◆ Choose someone who challenges you at least a little, but still seems in tune with your basic philosophy. If you've got the time and the money, you can even work with two or three brokers. It can help to hear different viewpoints.

Other advantages of landing a good broker at a full-service firm: Their relationship with you will likely induce them to do you additional favors from time to time, such as looking after a parent's investment account even if it's relatively small. And they can monitor complicated transactions, cutting down on administrative hassle.

What If You Still Want Someone to Talk To?

Suppose you don't have the assets to attract a super-broker, but still want someone knowledgeable to talk to before buying or selling. What then?

First, consider *why* you feel this way. For example, surveys have found that many women defer to men on financial decisions, even when they've got the smarts to learn good investing. My advice: it's worth enduring a little discomfort if the end result is to strengthen your independence.

Maybe you feel you make better decisions when you can bounce ideas off someone, rather than work in a vacuum. A great option might be to join a reputable investment club; see Appendix B for more information about such clubs.

Second, if you want to get advice about your overall portfolio, not just stock-picking, you can also consider hiring a *fee-only* financial planner, if you can find a good one who believes in stock-picking as well as asset allocation. Financial planners can't buy and sell shares on their own, so you'll still need a discount brokerage to actually handle trades. Appendix B lists further resources for finding certified planners.

> **Ⓢ Market Speak**
>
> A **fee-only** financial planner doesn't make money on commissions for selling financial products such as annuities or funds, and thus can honestly say they offer unbiased advice. A **fee-based** planner sounds similar, but in fact, they may be making commissions in addition to their fee, whether or not they tell you.

And third, if you finish reading this book and conclude you truly don't have the aptitude or time required to be a successful do-it-yourself investor, don't make the mistake of automatically throwing yourself into the arms of a full-service broker. A much better option is to avoid individual stocks and invest in indexed mutual funds instead. You'll need to learn something about asset allocation. You'll learn more about this in the next chapter, but you'll also want to look at the resources listed in Appendix B.

Picking a Good Discount Broker

As must be clear by now, our suggestion for most of you is to go with a discount broker, unless you've got hefty assets and plenty of time to search for an exceptional advisor.

Picking a good discounter is fairly straightforward. Again, the annual *SmartMoney* survey at www.smartmoney.com is a starting place. The magazine is reputable, and the survey itself is well constructed. It'll help you narrow down the possibilities to a few top candidates. To help make your final choice, visit their websites and call them directly with any questions you have.

Many of the premium discounters will be trying to woo you with special offers for opening an account—a bunch of free trades, a PDA or other gadget, even free memberships at golf courses around the country. But don't get distracted by such gimmicks. More important things to think about include the following:

Reasonably low commissions. Don't feel obligated to go for the lowest prices possible, such as the $5 trades offered by a few of the bottom-of-the-well deep discounters. These ultra-low commissions frequently come with strings attached, such as cranky, hard-to-use websites.

Customer service. Very important when you consider that you won't have your own personal financial advisor to track down problems. You want a friendly voice and a helpful answer on the other end of the line, not someone who doesn't have a clue or puts you on hold.

Investment advice. As noted, firms such as E*TRADE and Schwab have started offering advice via questionnaires and phone consults. These packaged perspectives may be helpful at times, but don't regard them as equivalent to a real relationship with a financial advisor or planner.

Research and tools. These include web-based tools for record-keeping and portfolio analysis, as well as access to selected news feeds and market analysis. Nice, but not absolutely essential, given that you'll probably want other sources of information besides. We'll talk more about this in Chapter 6.

Mutual-fund selection. Because mutual funds are a good way to diversify even if you like to pick stocks, be sure to check out which lines of funds the discounter offers. Of course, you can always buy funds elsewhere, but it doesn't hurt to keep your accounts as few as possible to cut down on hassle.

> **Red Flags**
>
> What if you've already got a broker-age account, but you're not happy with the firm? In that case, you can open an account at a new firm and transfer your assets, but the process can be a hassle. Try to keep things simple. Avoid liquidations, close out margin debt first, and make sure the new account is the same type as the old one. The Securities and Exchange Commission offers helpful tips at www.sec.gov/investor/pubs/acctxfer.htm.

Key Questions When Setting Up Your Account

After you've chosen your broker, creating an account involves (what else?) filling out a lot of paperwork, or possibly online forms. As part of this process, you'll need to make a couple of decisions:

Do you want a margin account? A margin account lets you borrow money based on the value of your stocks. On the plus side, the interest rates are generally attractive. And it's the only type of account that lets you sell stocks short, if you ever want to try that strategy (see Chapter 9 for a description). On the negative side, if the value of your stocks falls below a preset level, you'll have to immediately repay your broker. If you don't abuse credit, it's probably safe to opt for the margin account.

Do you want checking or bill-paying features?
Many people treat their brokerage account like a
bank account. It's easy to do, especially because any
cash sitting idle earns interest at money-market
rates. But I'd advise you to use your investment
account for investing, and keep a separate bank
account as you always have for everyday expenses.
Not having everything mushed together will make
it easier to keep track of your results.

The Bottom Line

Actually, you *can* buy stocks without a
broker—by buying them directly from the
issuing company. With a direct purchase
program, also known as a direct stock purchase plan, you can buy as little as a single share to start with. With a dividend
reinvestment program, or DRIP, you can
reinvest dividends from stock you already
own by buying more shares. Either way,
you pay only a small administrative fee or
no fee at all. The catch? Not all companies offer these programs. After you've
decided you like a stock and want to buy
it, check the company website.

Funding Your Account

You'll need to put some money into your new
account before you can begin buying stocks. You
can do this through any of the following means:

Write a check. This is the easiest method for getting started.

Transfer assets from another investment account. Transfers are prone to snags, which can mean hassles and lost time. And be extra careful about transferring funds from an IRA or 401(k). You'll want to keep these in a retirement account to avoid taxes for premature withdrawal, so be sure to tell your broker; he'll have you fill out the required paperwork.

Direct deposit. If you want to regularly feed cash into your investment account to facilitate investing, you can set up automatic deductions from your paycheck. If you're self-employed, you can do more or less the same thing with electronic bank transfers. In both cases, ask your broker for the forms.

Placing Orders

Actually placing orders is a fairly straightforward process, but you need to be careful each and every time. If you're buying or selling online, double-check or even triple-check the form you've filled out before confirming. When ordering by phone, write the order down first, then read it out loud to your broker or customer service representative, and then ask him to repeat it back to you and compare what he says to your notes. (Brokerage firms often tape these conversations, so if you're the one who makes a mistake, it will be at your own expense.)

Bids and Asks, and Why You Should Care

Before we get to the types of orders you can place, you'll need to understand the difference between a *bid* and an *ask* (also known as an *offer*). Think of an auction: someone who wants to buy places a *bid*; someone who wants to sell is *asking* a certain price.

On a stock exchange, middlemen of various sorts keep inventories of shares handy to facilitate trading. These middlemen are the ones who actually determine bid and ask prices, both to keep trading going and to make a profit for themselves by exploiting the gap in price between the bid and the ask.

This gap is known as the *spread*, and it exists because you must buy high at the ask price, but sell low at the bid price, with the middleman collecting the difference. Novice investors don't always realize it, but the spread is an additional cost to trading, over and above commissions.

The spread hurts you most if you buy and then sell within a very short time, such as a day. (Which, of course, you'll never do, because you're learning to be an investor, not a gambler.) For example, if you bought 500 shares of Cisco Systems at the ask of $19.37, then immediately sold it at the bid of $19.35, you'd lose 2 cents a share, for a total loss of $10 in addition to commissions. Fortunately for long-term investors, this cost is trivial compared to what you hope to earn through dividends and appreciation.

Different Types of Stock Orders

Whether you're ordering by phone or via a computer screen, the different types of orders let you specify the conditions under which you're willing to buy and sell.

Market order. This is the type of order you'll use most often; it tells your broker to buy or sell for you as soon as possible, at whatever the current market price is. Assuming your order is relatively small (which it almost certainly is, compared to the blocks of stock being tossed around by the big *institutional investors*), and assuming the stock is traded fairly often, your order will be filled extremely quickly—quickly enough that the price will likely be very close to the price you were just looking at on your online trading screen. Even so, you'll want to enter market orders as *day* orders only. This means that if it's not executed by the close of trading, it's canceled. The opposite of a day order is a *good-till-canceled* order, which stays alive until it's filled or you cancel it.

Limit orders. Limit orders tell your broker to buy for a specified price or less, or sell for a specified price or more. If the stock doesn't reach that price, the order isn't executed; if it does reach that price, the order is executed as soon as possible. Under most conditions, that means you buy for a tad less than specified, or sell for just a tad more. Limit orders can be more expensive than market orders, depending on your broker, but they're useful if either the stock or the market is especially volatile.

I recommend entering limit orders as day orders, too, for more flexibility and fewer headaches. A day order will be automatically cancelled at the end of that day's trading if you haven't made your buy or sell by then.

> 💲 **Market Speak**
>
> An **institutional investor** is a pension fund, mutual fund, university, bank, insurance company, or other behemoth. They have so much cash that it's nearly impossible for them to buy and sell stocks without making a very loud noise indeed. Nor can they easily invest in very small companies, however promising. It's like an elephant trying to hide in a shoebox. This gives you as an individual investor at least a theoretical advantage, because you can park your little dab of money in those same small companies without causing much excitement.

Stop orders. Stop orders are often used when selling, either to lock in a profit or to prevent further losses. You specify a certain price at which to sell (or less commonly, buy); when the stock hits this price, your broker enters a market order. Unlike a limit order, there are no restrictions set on price. If the market has chosen that day to go into a crash dive, you may wind up selling for far less than the trigger price you specified.

Stop-limit orders. These attempt to combine the best features of limit orders and stop orders. You set a trigger price for buying or selling, just as with a stop order, but at that point your order turns into a limit order rather than a market order. Again, your broker will sell for that price or better, or buy for that price or better. Stop-limit orders are handy when you're sure you want to make a certain trade at a certain price, but you're going on vacation and won't be able to monitor your portfolio. Enter it as "good-till-canceled," but make sure to cancel it on your return to civilization.

The Least You Need to Know

- You need a broker to buy and sell stock; you can't do it yourself, except with the direct investment programs offered by a handful of companies.

- For the do-it-yourself investor, a good discount brokerage will save you money on commissions.

- If you've got $1 million or more to invest, however, you can shop around for one of the few really good stock pickers who happen to work at the full-service firms.

- If you don't have a lot to invest but still want to talk stock decisions over, consider an investment club or a certified fee-only financial planner.

- Market orders, limit orders, stop orders, and stop-limit orders let you set different price conditions under which you're willing to buy or sell.

5

Planning Your Portfolio

In This Chapter

- Risk versus return
- Why diversify?
- Portfolio theory versus stock-picking
- Re-evaluating your portfolio

Way back in 1928, investment guru Philip L. Carret gave this warning: "It is the first principle of sound investment to diversify, not to put all one's eggs in one basket." Talk to any investment advisor today, and he'll tell you essentially the same thing.

But if it's such good advice, why do so many individual investors continue to ignore it?

The Wall Street Journal, in 2002, told the story of one such investor, a mid-level employee at Alteon WebSystems Inc. In the midst of the Internet bubble in 1999, Alteon went public. Its shares shot up in value, to the point that a year later, the employee's shares were worth more than $10 million. It was the only stock he owned, but so what?

He began making plans to retire, to spend more time with his kids, to go back to school. Meanwhile, his relatives, colleagues, and broker were telling him to safeguard his new-found wealth by diversifying—advice he failed to heed.

The sad end of the story is that the Internet bubble burst, and the employee's shares (now Nortel Networks shares, following a stock swap) plummeted in value. By the time he finally lost hope and sold, his paper millions had dwindled to only $400,000.

By placing all his bets on one horse, our hero took huge risks, earned a huge return, and then threw it away. The same blind faith that won him the money also lost it for him. In this chapter, you'll learn more about the slippery relationship between risk and return. Then we'll talk about how to avoid the one-horse mentality, in part by balancing your stock-picking with other assets in an overall investment portfolio.

Diversification and Risk

The fundamental idea behind diversification is that it reduces risk. But when it comes to stocks and other investments, not all risks are the same.

Two Kinds of Trouble

In particular, we need to distinguish between two kinds of risk: one narrow, the other broad.

- ◆ A company's stock can drop in price for any number of reasons—a corporate scandal, poor earnings, and so on. The company can even go out of business, although this is less common.

- ◆ Because of bad news of one sort or another, the stock market as a whole can drop, affecting all or nearly all stocks. Even markets in other countries can be hurt, because of the global economy.

You can see that of these two types, the first is more easily reduced by diversification than the second. Owning 20 stocks rather than just 1 reduces the risk of being hurt by any single company's troubles; likewise, owning 200 stocks is less risky than owning 20 stocks.

We can measure this kind of risk by tracking volatility. An investment whose returns are scattered all over the dartboard is considered more volatile, and thus riskier, than an investment whose returns are grouped close together.

The actual calculation used to measure volatility is called the *standard deviation*. For example, the standard deviation for the annual return of domestic stocks has typically run somewhere around 20 percent, whereas the standard deviation for long-term bonds is less than half that, about 9 percent. It's a no-brainer to conclude that for the years in question, stocks were riskier than bonds, but also offered better returns.

> ### ⑤ Market Speak
> The most commonly used measure of volatility comes from statistics, and goes by the name of **standard deviation**. Imagine a graph showing a bunch of gains or losses over a period of months or years for a stock. The standard deviation is a single number describing how widely scattered these returns are. A stock that shoots up and down a lot will have a high standard deviation.

Correlation and Noncorrelation

So far, diversification seems like nothing more than common sense. But it's actually more complicated than that.

Suppose you own 20 stocks, so you're feeling pretty good about being diversified. But let's suppose these are all energy-related stocks, meaning the companies are all affected by similar economic factors, such as energy prices, weather patterns, and so on.

If the economic climate is good for energy companies, these stocks will all tend to go up as a group. But if the economic climate is bad, they're all going to go down as a group. Guess what? You're not as diversified as you thought!

According to what's known in the investing world as *modern portfolio theory*, we call the tendency of stocks or other financial assets to move in tandem with each other *correlation*. Assets that follow each other's movements closely have high correlation; assets that zig and zag at random when compared to each other have low correlation. To be truly diversified, you want the least correlation possible, other things being equal.

> **Market Speak**
>
> **Modern portfolio theory,** which describes the role of standard deviation and correlation in portfolios, was developed in 1952 by Nobel laureate Harry Markowitz. More recent research has produced wrinkles and doubts, but many in the financial services world still preach the original as dogma. Regardless, don't think you have to learn pros and cons of portfolio theory to invest in stocks. Nothing could be further from the truth.

What Portfolio Purists Have to Say About Stock Pickers

Here's the rub: in its purest sense, portfolio theory holds that you can't beat the market by picking stocks. In fact, stock pickers are expected to do considerably worse than the market average.

According to portfolio theory, not only are all investors perfectly rational, but all the information about a company is so quickly distributed that everyone soon knows it. Therefore, the market is so efficient that a stock's current price is always the correct price. If you try to beat this efficient market by picking stocks, you incur unnecessary trading costs and increase your risk, while gaining nothing in return.

You'll hear this story from many advisors in the financial services industry, and you'll hear it even more from *critics* of the financial services industry! To bolster their argument, these critics cite statistics showing that the vast majority of mutual fund managers and other professional stock pickers do worse than the market average in the long run.

> **Bulls & Bears**
>
> When the statistics came in, the computer runs said the portfolios assembled by professionals were doing no better than randomly chosen portfolios of stocks. All that buying and selling and phoning around was for naught. Tack up the stock page on the wall; a monkey with a handful of darts can do just as good a job as that ad in the three-piece suit from the Stanford Business School.
>
> —Adam Smith, from *Paper Money* (Summit Books, 1981)

Rather than pick stocks, the theorists say, you should instead pick the right mix of risky, high-return instruments and low-risk, low-return instruments. "The right mix" varies depending on your financial goals, but generally it involves low-cost mutual funds that track an index such as the S&P 500, along with some bonds and real estate.

This tactic is called *asset allocation*, and it makes a good deal of sense. For example, the younger you are, the more risk you can tolerate in pursuit of high returns. Conversely, the closer to retirement you are, the less risk you tolerate, given that you don't have enough earning years left to compensate. Plus, keeping your costs low is always a great idea.

In fact, some form of asset allocation by itself will do just fine as a strategy if you finish this book and decide you don't have the time or inclination to pursue stock investing directly. But what if you're a stock picker? Are the portfolio theorists right that you don't have a chance? Keep reading!

What Stock Pickers Have to Say About Portfolio Purists

Fortunately, that's not all there is to the story. In fact, there are numerous holes in portfolio theory—some of which you can exploit if you're a disciplined investor willing to do your research.

Hole #1: It's fairly obvious that investors *aren't* all rational, and thus that the stock market isn't perfectly efficient. Both institutional and individual investors continue to make the same mistakes they always have. Individuals, for example, tend to trade too often and hold on to losers too long—behaviors that are purely psychological in origin.

Hole #2: Managers at the big mutual funds are handicapped. They nearly always have to stay fully invested in the market, just so they can run their fund. This is true even if market conditions are lousy and the stocks they're looking at are mediocre. As a small investor, you can afford to buy only when you think you've found a great stock, or even stay out of the market entirely, if you think conditions aren't right to invest.

Hole #3: There are too many examples of top investors beating the market average to ignore. Warren Buffett is perhaps the most famous example, but there are others, such as Bill Miller, head of the Legg Mason Value Trust. Portfolio theorists attempt to dismiss these legends as aberrations, instead of focusing on *why* they're successful.

How to Practice Asset Allocation and Still Pick Stocks

Here are my suggestions for how to diversify your assets, in the context of also being an investor in individual stocks:

Put some of your stock money into a mutual fund. Normally, you'd need at least 30 stocks to ensure adequate diversification within that asset class—but it's tough to keep track of even 10 stocks, as you'll learn in later chapters. The solution is to put some of your stock money in an indexed mutual fund—super-diversification at a low cost.

Diversify within domestic stocks. You can pick stocks from different *sectors* to gain some zig and zag. Or you can pick stocks from different-size companies—some large, some medium, some small—for additional diversification. The more diverse your individual stock holdings, the less money you need in that indexed mutual fund, and vice versa. Keep in mind, though, that you don't buy a stock just because it offers diversification— you need other compelling reasons besides.

Consider non–U.S. stocks or mutual funds. Foreign stocks offer varying degrees of diversification: you get only moderate diversification with stocks from developed countries, such as France or Japan, as opposed to much more with stocks from emerging markets such as Taiwan and China. Of course, these latter stocks are riskier, too. But that means they also can offer higher returns.

($) Market Speak _____

A term beloved by market pundits, **sector** or **market sector** means a set of businesses in similar industries, such as the high-tech sector, which includes the software industry and the hardware industry. As you've seen in discussion about the idea of correlation, stocks belonging to the same sector tend to move up and down together in response to the same economic forces. You can diversify your stocks according to sector, and you can also buy mutual funds that represent individual sectors.

Look at assets in the context of your total net worth. Not just stocks and bonds, but your home and your debt, including mortgage and credit cards—even your projected future income. If you're like most investors, your house will be your biggest asset. This is a good way to keep the size of your stock holdings in perspective.

Break your portfolio into subsets. First, look at stocks only; next, stocks plus mutual funds; then all publicly traded investments, including bonds and cash; and last, your total net worth. The smaller subsets, such as stocks or stocks plus mutual funds, need to be reviewed more often than the larger subsets. Stocks should be reviewed at least quarterly, whereas your total net worth can be reviewed annually. Look at each subset as a percentage of the total portfolio to check whether the allocation continues to make sense, given the risks and rewards.

Use the "100 minus your age" rule of thumb for stocks. It's just a starting point, but it's a reasonable one. Excluding your home, the percent you can afford to have invested in stocks is roughly equal to 100 minus your age. So, for example, a 28-year-old could think in terms of investing 72 percent of his funds in stocks.

Take advantage of online tools for portfolio analysis. For example, Morningstar (at www.morningstar.com) has a highly rated portfolio analyzer.

Thinking About Risk

When you review the risks in your portfolio, think especially hard about risks that may affect all of your assets at one time.

Here's an example. The Boston area, where I live, is home to many large mutual-fund companies. Because of this, demand for my house (and therefore its market value) is at least somewhat affected by the stock market. In other words, my exposure to equities is higher than it at first appears.

Here's a similar example. If you work for a drug company, you may not want to own a lot of drug stocks, especially because your company may already give you a lot of ownership through contributions of stock to your 401(k). Your job is subject to the same risks as the stock.

Get Outside the Software Box

Portfolio analysis software can be a very helpful tool, but you don't have to always accept the packaged definitions for what stocks fit into which categories. Suppose you think IBM has stopped being a technology company and is now a business services company. If so, move it into that sector and reassess your allocation accordingly.

Likewise, if you see a likely correlation among your holdings that doesn't fit into the standard categories, make up a category of your own and see how your risk looks when sliced that way. For instance, if you've noticed that a lot of your stocks have a high proportion of international sales, you'll have a lot of exposure to strength or weakness in the dollar.

> ▶ **Red Flags**
>
> Many financial advisors use special software programs to suck in your financial data, digest it, and then spit out an extremely precise asset allocation based on your risk tolerance—all the way down to the half-percentage point. But beware: this technique has severe limitations. For starters, asset allocation relies heavily on historic returns, and as we all know, historic returns describe the past perfectly, but the future poorly. Therefore, any attempt at computerized precision is a waste of resources, no matter how nice the printout looks.

Think also about how *much* risk you're comfortable taking. Remember, it's not unusual for the market to fall 10 percent in a year. Are you okay if you lose that much on your portfolio or even more on an individual investment? Are you okay with even bigger risks if they give you the potential for even bigger returns? As mentioned in Chapter 1, be honest with yourself about your comfort level and how nervous or calm you've been about big investments in the past.

Break Out Your Crystal Ball

Okay, so now you know your respective allocations along various categories of risk and return. How do you judge whether your exposures to risk in these categories are good or bad—in particular, whether you're overinvested or underinvested in stocks?

Here's a short answer. If your overall interpretation of the market and the economy tells you that stocks are good to own for the next few years, you're happy if your exposure is high. But if your reading of the signs and portents tells you that stocks are much riskier than usual to own, you'd rather have less exposure—perhaps much less.

For example, if you think we are at the start of an economic recovery, you might be comfortable with a relatively high percentage of your portfolio invested in value stocks. But if you think we are near the peak of an economic cycle, and that things might be about to stall or turn down, you might want to reduce your exposure to stocks.

A lot depends on how soon you anticipate needing the money. For example, the closer you are to retirement, the more you'll want to safeguard your existing net worth. That again means paying attention to whether the market is overvalued, whether the economy is perking or peaking, and so on. You don't care whether stocks have returned x percent over the past however many decades; you care about what they're most likely to do in the next few years.

It's a hard thing to gauge economic and market conditions with an eye to the future, but better to make the attempt than to rely on the false comfort of long-term historic returns.

An example of when it would have made sense to reduce your exposure was during the height of the Internet bubble, when stocks in general had become overpriced to anyone willing to pay attention to the fundamentals.

However, big shifts in or out of the market should still be relatively infrequent events. If you find yourself doing it a lot, you're in danger of trying to time the market. This is almost always a losing strategy for the individual investor.

Thinking About Returns

Speaking of historic returns for stocks, something you need to keep in mind is that the future may not be as rosy as the past.

First, remember that the U.S. stock market has only returned 10 percent per year over the last 80 years—not 15 or 20 percent. And many market experts think that 10 percent may be on the high side going forward, given the low interest rates we've been seeing.

Past Glory, Future Uncertainty

Some researchers have gone so far as to say that certain factors probably pushed stock prices up in decades past, but won't be doing so in the future. These factors include the following:

High transaction costs. Prior to the past 20 or so years, commissions and account fees were quite high—meaning that actual returns were lower than might appear. Now that costs are lower, the theory goes, returns will drop to keep suit.

Price pressure from institutional investors. As the perception of stocks as risky investments has lessened over the past 40 years, pension plans and other institutional investors have hopped on board, increasing demand. Now these investors are fully stocked up, so they're no longer driving up prices.

Declines in capital gains and dividend taxes. As these taxes dipped, they made stocks more attractive, again increasing demand. But today, stocks are about as tax-attractive as they're likely to get.

Keeping Your Head Straight

Although stocks will likely remain a good investment for years to come, you'll want to keep your stock-picking expectations realistic. Here are some tips for doing so:

Expect a little less. If you expect an 8 percent return from stocks and instead earn 10 percent, you'll be pleased.

Set your minimum goal as beating the returns on your savings account. This is the approach that hedge funds use when setting fees.

Don't get upset if you fail to beat the market average every year. Remember Bill Miller, of the Legg Mason Value Trust? He's earned a reputation as one of the very top money managers for beating the market 14 years in a row. Most other money managers are ecstatic if they manage this trick a mere *five* years in a row.

Don't think all your picks have to be right. It's like batting averages: no one bats a thousand. Don't try to be perfect, just try to get better.

What About Rebalancing?

Say you're 30, with your best wage-earning years still ahead of you. You've decided you're comfortable with putting 75 percent of your relatively small investing portfolio into stocks. One of these stocks is Baby Balloons, a small but well-managed company that dominates the recently popular hot-air balloon market for toddlers. Demographic research has convinced you that more and more young parents today want their kids to fly, meaning the company may be posed for serious growth.

It turns out you're right, and Baby Balloons has a truly spectacular year. By year end, this stock alone has so outpaced the rest of your portfolio that stocks now account for 82 percent of your assets. Does this mean you should sell some of your sky-high stock to push your allocation back into balance?

It depends on who you talk to—a dyed-in-the-wool portfolio theorist, or a stock picker.

Rebalancing in Theory

Portfolio theory relies on a tactic known as *rebalancing* to make sure you get the best overall return for a given level of risk. To rebalance, you sell assets that have increased in value and buy assets that have stayed the same or gone down in value, restoring your allocation's original ratios.

Paradoxically, this strategy can also improve returns. Portfolio purists are fond of examples showing how certain allocations would have out-performed the S&P 500 over one decade or another, simply through rebalancing each year. The secret is that you're forced to sell on the way up and buy on the way down—a contrarian strategy that spells success over the long term.

The Bottom Line

For the period from 2000 through 2004, if you'd held a $10,000 portfolio split evenly between stocks and bonds, a simple buy-and-hold strategy would have seen your assets grow to $12,638 at the end of the 10-year period, with an annualized rate of return of roughly 4.8 percent. But what if you'd rebalanced each year to maintain your 50-50 split between asset classes? Your assets would have grown an additional $1,845, reaching a total of $14,483, at an annualized rate of return of roughly 7.7 percent! Why? Because market swings would have forced you to periodically sell high-performing assets and buy low-performing assets—no matter how much your instincts protested.

Getting back to Baby Balloons, if you followed portfolio theory to the letter, you would indeed sell off stocks to get back to your original 72 percent allocation. But does rebalancing really make sense in the context of stock-picking—an activity that portfolio theorists regard as futile to begin with?

Rebalancing in Reality

The fact is, if you're committed to investing in individual stocks, you must take a very different approach to selling. If you're comfortable that the market is a good place for you to be, then you're going to ride your individual stocks according to your underlying investing philosophy.

If you're a *value investor*, for example, you're going to want to hang on to a good value stock as long as you think the company and its business are sound and the long-term story is that the stock price is bound to go up. If one of your stocks zooms up, but your analysis shows it's not yet overvalued, you're not going to sell it just to rebalance!

> **(S) Market Speak**
>
> If you're a **value investor,** you specialize in good companies temporarily out of favor, or companies whose earnings or assets aren't yet fully reflected in their stock prices. You'll learn more about value investing in Chapter 6.

Instead, you sell if you think the stock or the market in general has become too overvalued, or if new information about the business or industry makes you think the company isn't going to do as well going forward.

In the case of Baby Balloons, you never stopped researching, even when the stock took off. Now, an obscure industry newsletter alerts you to product liability issues that may spell trouble for the company in a few months. At the same time, other investors keep piling on board, continuing to drive up the stock—to the point that it's looking overpriced compared to underlying value. Rather than try and guess when the balloon will pop, you decide to sell now and preserve your profits.

Avoiding Disaster

There's another reason to sell, too: if you have such a huge winner that the risk of losing it all would be catastrophic. Remember the beginning of the chapter, where we talked about the employee whose Alteon WebSystems stock had grown to a value of $10 million? Regardless of how well he thought Alteon would do in the future, he should have diversified his new-found wealth into other holdings to protect it.

Here are two things I (Theresa) often tell investors in this regard: first, don't invest more in any single opportunity than you can afford to lose; and second, if an investment has you so worried you can't sleep, it's time to sell. Hanging on to a situation that fills you with dread is never worth it.

Remember, though, that your overall asset allocation depends on your take on the markets and the economy, not on concerns about individual stocks. If you find that appreciation has increased your exposure to stocks to a level you're not comfortable with, you should probably take steps to reduce that exposure.

You'll learn much more about all of this in Chapter 9. For now, just keep in mind that for the stock investor, asset allocation is an elastic affair, not a rigid set of rules.

The Least You Need to Know

- ◆ Diversification reduces the risk of owning stocks.

- ◆ Ways to diversify include increasing the number of stocks you own, picking stocks from different industries, and investing in assets such as bonds or real estate.

- ◆ Asset allocation is the practice of setting specific targets for diversification, designed to balance overall risk versus overall return.

- ◆ Modern portfolio theory holds that asset allocation is all, stock-picking worse than nothing.

- ◆ When reviewing your allocations, pay attention both to individual stocks and to your exposure to stocks in general.

6

Investment Styles

In This Chapter

- ◆ Value versus growth
- ◆ Other investment styles
- ◆ Three great investors
- ◆ Setting your style

My stock-picking style fits my personality: cautious and a bit on the pessimistic side. Maybe it's because I grew up in the 1970s, the downbeat decade of Vietnam, Watergate, and the oil embargo.

Your style as an investor is almost certain to reflect your character as well—perhaps more than you'd think. That's just fine, because people have done well with many different styles. There are value-oriented investors like me, bargain hunters who look for stocks that are undervalued now. Then there are growth investors, glass-half-full types who look for stocks with bold prospects for the future.

Most people, myself included, aren't 100 percent one style or the other. In fact, it's not always possible to draw hard-and-fast lines between growth and value. Many seasoned investors don't bother to try; they simply characterize their style as a blend of value and growth.

But value, growth, and the various combinations thereof all have one thing in common: they rely on gathering and analyzing fundamental information about the company behind the stock.

Another group of investing styles goes a different route, eschewing fundamental research to focus instead on patterns in stock prices, market volume, and other data. These approaches, collectively known as technical analysis, often rely on mathematical and statistical models in an effort to predict the future.

Although some avowed practitioners of technical analysis have made a lot of money, I believe their success is most likely based either on short-term luck or an integration of technical and fundamental analysis.

To be blunt, I don't see how it's possible to have an investment style without first having the facts about the companies in which you invest. How are sales and profits? Is there a dividend? Are new products in the pipeline? What's the competition? And so on and so on.

In this chapter, we take a closer look at all the investing styles previously mentioned, so you can decide for yourself what makes sense. The chapter rounds things off with a brief look at three successful stock investors whose examples may help guide you in finding a style of your own.

Value Versus Growth

Although they're often pitted against one another, like football teams or heavyweight boxers, I think of value and growth as different ways of looking at the same information—not opposite sides of a stock-picking slugfest.

Let's suppose you were considering buying shares in the Tribune Company. At the end of June 2005, the company's stock had lost more than a quarter of its value over the past 2 years, while the S&P 500 stocks overall gained more than 20 percent. One big reason was falling circulation at its flagship newspapers, the *Los Angeles Times*, *Newsday*, and the *Chicago Tribune*.

But even with declining readership, the company's newspapers were dominant in large markets, and continued to produce large amounts of cash. So the Tribune Company could be seen as a value investment, a company with underrated assets.

On the other hand, it also had elements of a growth business. For one thing, the company co-owned the WB television network with Time Warner, giving it a growing, non-newspaper business. And if it could become more adept at using the Internet, there might be hidden growth possible in the company's core business of content generation.

Sometimes you'll find a stock only a growth investor could love, such as a biotech firm with a promising new drug in development but no sales for years to come. Or one that's a value seeker's special—perhaps a venerable manufacturing firm that's been steadily losing sales to overseas companies, but still has business assets worth more than the stock price. More often, though, stocks (and investors) mix elements of both.

> **Red Flags**
>
> Value investors risk getting stuck with stocks that are cheap now, and destined to stay that way. Evaluating the quality of management and business operations is a key factor in avoiding these "value traps." Sure, the perennial number three maker of industrial fans may look underpriced on paper compared to numbers one and two. But is that because it's been overshadowed, or because it has inferior products or service? If it's the latter, earnings may never improve, as the only way the company can get business is by cutting prices. In that case, what appears to be an undervalued stock could really be no bargain.

Value

Value investors look at the present. They're looking for companies that are worth more right now than the market thinks they are. Often, value investors look for stocks with low prices relative to how much a company makes, or for high dividends or valuable business assets. Consider the following:

Low prices. In Chapter 7, we go through price/ earnings ratios, cash flow, and other ways of measuring a stock's price against the company's value. Crunching the numbers is at the heart of the value style. When you find a company that produces higher-than-average earnings per share, there's a good chance you've found a stock with room to rise.

High dividends. You also want to look at the company's dividend. Suppose it pays out 25 cents per quarter, or $1 a year. With the stock priced at $30, you'd be getting a 3.25 percent annual return on your investment just from the dividend alone. That's more than you're probably earning on your savings or money-market account.

Valuable assets. Finally, you need to know what else a company has going for (and against) it: how much debt, future business plans, the outlook for its industry, and so on. One basic measure is book value, a totaling up of all of a company's assets (cash, real estate, equipment, goodwill) minus all of its liabilities (loans, accounts payable, pension obligations, and the like).

Ultimately, you need to decide whether the stock is underpriced. For that, you want to use not one valuation measure, but all of these. As a value investor, you're looking for places the so-called efficient markets haven't reached by sorting out financial and business information for yourself.

Sometimes that means seeking out companies or types of businesses other investors aren't interested in, or trying to see through short-term bad news to find long-term strength. For example, cyclical industries subject to the ups and downs of the economy, such as automakers, airlines, or mining companies, can have long down periods. But beaten-down stocks that can't get a date to the prom have one big advantage: they tend to have low *betas*, meaning that they are less volatile than the market as a whole.

> (\$) **Market Speak**
>
> **Beta** is a way of describing how
> movements in a stock's price compare
> with those of the broader market. A beta of
> 1 means the stock tends to move up and
> down about as much as the market. A
> beta below 1 means it tends to move less,
> while a beta above 1 means it tends to
> move more. As you might expect, growth
> stocks often have betas above 1, meaning
> they're riskier than the market average.
> Value stocks, on the other hand, typically
> have betas lower than 1.

Growth

Growth investors look at the future. That is, they
start with broader social, economic, political, and
business trends and try to identify companies that
will benefit from them.

They're still using fundamentals, they look at the
same financial information as value investors. But
they're willing to pay more now—sometimes a lot
more—to get in on growth later. Consider the following:

Business insight. Because growth investors are
looking for potential, they're generally more interested in a company's business information than in its
financial data. Obviously, no investor can afford to
ignore unclear accounting, unsustainable losses, or

other signs of a financial debacle in the making. But if you're looking for the next Microsoft, it's also essential to know as much as you can about software.

Knowing where to look. Speaking of software, it's no coincidence that so many growth companies are clustered in technology, health care, and media. Growth investors tend to focus on companies with new products or the ability to tap new markets, which often means they look hardest at industries where innovation is in full swing.

Finding future value. This is what makes growth investing hard—you're always looking at new products and services, so there aren't any past financial results. Statistics tend not to be much use in finding growth stocks. By the time they show rapid growth, it's often nearing an end.

Almost no company can keep growing faster than those around it for more than a few years. Even the greatest growth businesses, from McDonald's to Intel, slow down eventually.

Unlike value investing, which relies more heavily on a company's financial information and existing business situation, growth investing requires you to judge a company's business prospects down the line, and be ready to move quickly as those projections change. And the betas of these stocks tend to be high, meaning that they're more volatile than most. That makes it the harder of the two styles, although the thrill of finding exciting new companies also makes it the more popular one.

The Bottom Line

Virtually every great growth stock becomes a value stock eventually. For example, let's look at McDonald's. For the 20 years from 1981 through 2000, the stock's value went from a split-adjusted share price of less than $2 all the way up to $34. Earnings grew explosively, due in large part to openings of new stores in Europe, South America, and Asia.

Eventually, the company ran out of places to expand. Management was slow to adjust, and a few years of continued emphasis on growth led to a first-ever money-losing year in 2003. When McDonald's share price dipped—going as low as $12 in March of that year—value investors got interested. At that price, the company's dividend was 1.9 percent, much better than the interest banks were offering at the time. With strong cash flow from more than half a million restaurants in the United States alone, McDonald's management had the time and resources to address the company's problems. A focus on improving existing restaurants, adjusting pricing, changing menus, and other business changes brought the business back to profitability, and management made clear its optimism by raising the dividend by 70 percent later in the year. And as of June 30, 2005, the stock price had risen again to more than $30 a share.

The Effect of the Economy

Investment styles don't exist in a vacuum. How well they work depends heavily on conditions in both the stock markets and the U.S. (and to a lesser extent, world) economy.

Value investing generally does better when the economy is just beginning to recover from a downturn. It's easier to find underpriced stocks when the economy isn't doing well, and to see your research rewarded as conditions improve.

Growth investing, on the other hand, generally does better later in the economic cycle, when the economy is expanding rapidly. That's when the earnings and cash flow growth the growth investor hoped for may actually start to appear on a company's balance sheet.

The perfect investor would probably adjust her style to suit economic conditions. You should, too. It doesn't have to be a radical shift. Simply taking into account the state of the economy as it relates to a stock you're considering can go a long way toward improving your decision making.

Socially Conscious Investing

A growing number of people have made ethics part of their investing style. The amount of money under professional management that includes some form of screening to eliminate unwanted types of businesses—or seek out desired ones—doubled between 1999 and 2005, to more than $2 trillion dollars.

Alcohol, tobacco, gambling, weapons, nuclear energy, and many other products and services are shunned by different people. On the other hand, companies involved in alternative energy, organic farming, or open-source software may be sought out.

You may find that socially conscious investing tilts you toward growth companies. That's because the types of industries that pass muster tend to be heavy in newer, faster-growing companies. For example, a video game design firm has less direct environmental impact and may be a more highly rated place to work compared to an auto parts maker.

Sometimes it's not what a company does but how it does it. A company's record on equal opportunity, environmental protection, or political involvement plays a key role for some investors.

Whatever your personal convictions, as a stock picker you're perfectly positioned to mesh them with your financial strategy. While you're doing your research, you'll be able to get an idea of where a business stands on issues you care about, and you can look elsewhere if you don't like what you learn.

Another alternative is to become a shareholder activist—seeking to change company policy from within. But writing letters, submitting issues for shareholder vote, and backing candidates for the board of directors can become a job in and of itself. It's hard to make an impact as just one investor— and it's certainly not for the easily discouraged or anyone with limited time.

Technical Analysis

Technical analysis dispenses with fundamental research and concentrates on market data. Practitioners believe the market is essentially inefficient and driven by human emotion, so that prices tend to move in trends.

They create charts tracking prices and volume (number of shares bought and sold) for individual stocks and for the markets. Then they try to find patterns, and base their trades on buying at low points and selling at highs within those patterns.

Technical analysts may look for resistance levels (prices at which a stock's upward momentum seems to stall) or support points (prices below which it seems reluctant to fall). If a stock has traded in a range between 81 and 94 for a quarter or two, a technical analyst might say it has support at 80 and resistance at 95.

Patterns in share prices can even take on colorful-sounding names. For example, let's say our hypothetical stock's price languished in the low $80s for a month, then rose into the $90s for a month before retreating back into the low $80s. The resulting chart, with low points (shoulders) on either side of a fairly wide high point (head) would be, you guessed it, a "head and shoulders" chart.

The appeal of this approach is obvious. How nice it would be to have a simple chart—or even a bunch of complicated ones—which could tell you where markets and individual stocks are headed.

The major problem, though, is that no such charts exist. For short periods, technical analysis may be able to accurately show how investor psychology is driving stock prices. Longer term, there's no evidence that it has proven predictive power.

There are technical analysts who have made money, though. As I said at the start of this chapter, I believe their success is most likely due to good fortune or, more likely, using a fundamental investing style in combination with technical analysis.

 The Bottom Line

Technical analysis has turned up one method that does seem to have predictive power. When investors think the markets are headed in one direction, they're often likely to go the opposite way. In other words, when everyone else thinks it's time to buy, it could actually be a good time to sell. One publication, *Market Vane*, actually surveys market newsletter writers each week. In the past, the more upbeat they have been, the more likely the market has been to go down.

Day Trading

Day trading is technical analysis on steroids. Using online brokerage accounts, day traders often buy and sell a stock within a few hours, minutes, or even seconds. Their game plan is to use technical analysis to get in at a low point in a stock's trading pattern, and get out just a bit higher.

In addition to the lack of fundamental information or economic analysis, day traders also have to beat high costs: constant trading racks up commissions, even at the lowest-cost Internet sites. To achieve the volume to make small profit margins add up, some day traders borrow money, often by buying on margin. Although this can multiply profits, it does the same for losses—and adds interest and transaction expenses, too.

Day trading looks more like gambling than investing to me. Although it may be a workable style for a few driven types with a high tolerance for volatility and a keen feel for trading, I strongly suspect even they could do better by incorporating fundamental research. Perhaps some of the truly successful ones do.

Three Great Investors

All three of the men profiled in this section produced handsome returns for investors, beating average stock market returns over a decade or more. All relied on extensive fundamental research to find stocks worth buying. But each was looking for different types of companies.

All three are (or were) managers of mutual funds. Although many successful investors run private investment funds or simply manage their own money, only mutual-fund managers must report their results in public. This makes their performance easy to track and the differences in their investing styles plain to see.

The Bottom Line

How much difference does better-than-average performance make? Earning and reinvesting an additional 1 percent on a $10,000 investment adds up over 10 years to an extra $1,046. Adding 2 percent translates to $2,190, 3 percent to $3,439, and so on. As you can see, even relatively small-sounding percentage gains can add up to large amounts in real dollars.

John Neff

John Neff ran the Vanguard Windsor Fund from 1964 through his retirement in 1995. His fund outperformed the Standard & Poor's 500 Index in 22 of those 31 years, and returns averaged about 3 percent higher than the S&P over that time.

Neff was a value investor, or as he liked to say, a "low P/E investor," who liked checking out the list of stocks hitting new lows each day. He was well aware that most of the companies on it deserved to be there, and was looking for the few that didn't.

One measure he looked for was a combination of dividends and expected business growth adding up to at least double a stock's price-to-earnings ratio. Think about that: if a stock had a P/E of 10, Neff wanted to see dividend yield and expected future earnings growth add up to at least 20.

One of Neff's classic value picks came with Ford, in 1984. With the U.S. auto industry hit hard by Japanese imports, Neff chose to invest heavily in Ford stock. The possibility of bankruptcy was scaring investors, and Ford's P/E had fallen to just 2.5.

John Train, in his book *Money Masters of Our Time*, reports that Neff liked the unpretentious style of Ford's management. But he also presumably liked the numbers. Ford had a dividend yield of 5 percent, swollen by the drop in the stock price, so that Neff was meeting his double P/E requirement based on the dividend alone!

Research helped Neff see through the emotions to the underlying value. Of course, a high dividend wouldn't have lasted long if the company was really going under. But he noted that Ford management had actually raised the dividend early in the year, indicating confidence in the company's outlook.

Introduction of new products and cost cutting at Ford proved his judgment correct. Train puts Neff's average price paid for Ford at less than $14 per share. Three years later, the stock was at $50, and Neff's fund had a profit (at least on paper) of almost $500 million.

Bulls & Bears

> Low P/E ratio stocks populate bargain basements because their underlying earnings and growth prospects don't excite most investors. As a low P/E investor, you have to distinguish misunderstood and overlooked stocks selling at bargain prices from many more stocks with lackluster prospects.
>
> —John Neff, from his book *John Neff on Investing* (Wiley, 1999)

Tom Marsico

Founder of the Marsico Funds mutual-fund company in 1997 and manager of the Janus Twenty Fund for almost 10 years prior to that, Tom Marsico bettered the average returns of the S&P 500 stocks by an average of 4.5 percent over the 17 years from 1987 through 2004.

Marsico is a growth investor. He's looking for companies with new and innovative products and services or new market opportunities that can turbo-charge earnings. So, although a company's past performance and current financial statements matter, what's ahead matters more.

Marsico and his staff rely heavily on understanding the plans of a company's management and how those plans fit into changes in the world, whether it's the rise of the Internet or the expansion of China's economy. As you might expect, his results vary sharply. His flagship, Marsico Focus Fund, was up 51.3 percent in 1998, up 55.3 percent in 1999, then down 17.9 percent in 2000, and down another 20.8 percent in 2001.

One quintessential growth pick by Marsico was QUALCOMM, in 1999. QUALCOMM was a designer and maker of chips and other key cell phone components, and its CDMA technology became the standard for most current cell phones. The key here was the settlement of a long dispute over patents with Ericsson, announced in March 1999. The next month, Marsico invested at about $19 to $20 a share. The stock experienced a wild run-up, and Marsico ultimately exited with a profit of more than $300 million, according to Forbes.com.

Other successful picks for Marsico during this golden period for growth were digital storage–maker EMC and networking giant Cisco Systems; both illustrate his focus on leadership companies in new industries. When he found them, Marsico typically purchased these and other stocks at high P/E ratios relative to the average for the S&P 500, as well as high prices relative to other measures besides P/E.

Marsico's growth-focused style was a perfect fit with the Internet age. Here was real change, and a real opportunity for companies to create new businesses. But it's also worth noting that by the end of 2001, he'd sold many of his technology holdings, taken his lumps, and moved on to other areas of the market in search of better opportunities.

> ### Bulls & Bears
>
> Our goal is to find companies with sustainable top-line and bottom-line growth. Once we've identified leading companies in industries that may benefit from trends we foresee in the macroeconomic environment, we rank those companies. Then we further refine our list to top-tier companies with good managements in good businesses.
>
> —Tom Marsico, from the first Marsico Funds shareholder report

Bill Miller

Bill Miller has been sole manager of the Legg Mason Value Trust since 1990 (he was co-manager from 1982 to 1990). During the 14 years through 2004, this mutual fund outperformed the S&P 500 average every single year. Over the 10 years from 1995 to 2004, Miller outperformed the average by 6.1 percent annually.

Miller's style is a blend of growth and value. He's willing to buy companies in growing fields or expanding markets that carry P/E ratios value investors would reject. But he's also willing to buy undervalued firms in slower-growing areas.

In other words, Miller will take earnings growth wherever he can find it at a discounted price, whether it's a financial services firm undervalued due to the economic cycle or a technology company whose growth potential isn't yet reflected in its stock price.

A good example of Miller finding value in a growth stock comes from his pick of America Online in 1996.

At the time, AOL was being sued over failure to provide adequate server capacity for its users. With future earnings in doubt, many growth investors lost interest. And a business predicated heavily on future growth wasn't even on the screen for most value investors.

With the stock's price down more than 50 percent from its high, Miller and his team saw an opportunity to buy growth at a substantial discount, and did so. Their flexible approach was rewarded, as AOL stock more than doubled in the next year from its 1996 low.

Bulls & Bears

Most growth people own stocks that are secularly underpriced: things that can grow for long periods of time. Our portfolios historically tended to be ... better diversified along both cyclical and secular lines.

—Bill Miller, from an interview with SmartMoney.com

Setting Your Style

You may have noticed that all three of the investors I've used as examples had some notable similarities, despite their very different styles.

All relied on extensive fundamental research. All looked for future earnings or dividend growth—they wanted good fundamentals, not just good stories. And all based their decisions on rational evaluation and their own judgment, not on public opinion, market swings, or emotions.

Now, how about you? Do you see big possibilities for growth in national security spending? Under-valued consumer products companies? Rapid expansion ahead in fuel-cell technology? A small niche firm with a great business that hasn't gotten noticed yet?

I'd encourage you to follow your instincts, do your homework, and see where you wind up. That's the only real way to create an investing style of your own.

The Least You Need to Know

- ◆ Fundamental investing is an overall style based on research into individual companies, business areas, and economic conditions.
- ◆ Growth and value investing styles are opposite ends of the fundamental investing spectrum.

- Technical analysis is an investing style based on market patterns, not fundamental research; there's little evidence it works in the long term.

- Your personal stock selection style should incorporate fundamental research, ideas borrowed from successful investors, and your own instincts and judgment.

Doing Your Research Right

In This Chapter

- Keeping up with the world
- Panning for gold with a database
- Coming up with ideas
- Sources you can and can't trust
- Digging into a stock

If you can run a fantasy baseball league, plan a wedding, or shop for the very best deal on a new car, you can research stocks and companies. So why do so many individual investors buy first, and ask questions never?

Often, it's because they're too intimidated and don't even know where to begin. Just as often, they don't want the responsibility. Plus, many people believe investing is mostly luck. You wouldn't research a lottery ticket before buying it, so why research a stock?

This leads to conversations such as the following: "I'm into JetBlue. My broker suggested it."

"Shouldn't you learn a little about the airline indus- try first?" "Well, I flew on JetBlue once and really liked it. So I feel good about that."

Or this: "My friend Vickie says this biotech start- up invented a great new drug, so I bought 100 shares." "Okay, but where is the drug in the FDA approval process? Is this the company's only poten- tial product?" "I have no idea. But the stock's gone up since I bought it!"

I hope to persuade you to be different—to take your time and learn about a stock, the business behind it, and what the market thinks versus what you think. That's how you find and verify real opportunity in stocks.

In this chapter, we compare trustworthy versus untrustworthy information sources. We talk about how to spot interesting stocks, then how to dig into them further, picking up insights into the company and its industry. All of this is essential groundwork for Chapters 8 and 9 … so don't skip ahead!

Taking Care of Business News

To be an informed investor, you need to keep up with business news in general. And that's business news, not just stock market news—what's happen- ing in the economy, business-related regulation, trends in company earnings reports, and so on. Some news affects all companies, other news only certain industries.

Any major newspaper with a big business section is okay, but the industry standard here is the *Wall Street Journal*. If you like to read hard copy, subscribing to the print version is fine, as long as you can get it delivered that same day; otherwise, subscribe online at wsj.com.

If you have time, you can also subscribe to other general-interest business publications. *Forbes* is my favorite, but *Business Week* or *Fortune* would serve as well. Note that *Money* magazine won't do. It and similar magazines concentrate on financial planning and lifestyle, not on business and investing.

If you really become hooked, you may want to read daily publications targeted at stock junkies. *Investors Business Daily* is popular with many money managers and available in print and online; TheStreet.com is available online only.

Bulls & Bears

If you do what other people do, you get the results that other people get. So by diversifying your sources of information, you get insights, analogies and metaphors, and you see connections that other people might not see. That's a fruitful way to go about thinking about markets.

—Bill Miller, manager of the Legg Mason Value Trust Fund

Accessing the Stock Universe

Next, you want access to at least one reliable source of information about any and all companies and stocks—either a printed database or an online version of the same thing.

These databases offer summaries of nearly any public company you'd want to know about. You can get a quick idea of whether you'd be interested in investigating the stock further, as well as what the market thinks of the company's prospects, which will help you understand why the stock is priced the way it is.

What are your best sources here?

If you've got a full-service broker, this is the research you're paying for. Discount brokers such as Schwab also offer research, for a fee. Essentially, you call up your broker, tell him or her what you're interested in, and they do your legwork. They'll mail or e-mail you what they find.

Value Line is the best-known printed database; its one-page summaries are even popular with professional money managers. As with most databases, it covers primarily big, well-established companies. If you develop an interest in smaller companies, you may have to develop your own sources. You can also get it online, in which case it comes with a stock-screening tool. The big drawback to Value Line is that it costs upward of $500 a year. Fortunately, many libraries carry the print version.

Personally, my current favorite is the online stocks database that comes with a premium subscription to Morningstar.com. It's far cheaper than Value Line, and it, too, boasts a stock screener and many other tools. Other virtues are Morningstar's reputation for independence and the handy summaries of "Bulls Say" versus "Bears Say" market sentiments. And you'll get access to their well-known mutual fund research.

Also useful are *Hoover's*, expensive but sometimes available at the library, and *Standard & Poor's Stock Outlook*, ditto. Both are better on company descriptions than stock analysis.

Charts are another useful source of information. Even though I don't recommend the technical approach to stock-picking, as discussed in Chapter 6, charts of prices, earnings, dividends, and other fundamental information can give you a snapshot of the factors that have driven the price up or down. And it's an easy way to see whether a stock is a cyclical (moving up and down with the economy) or a growth stock.

Short-term charts are available from Daily Graphs at www.dailygraphs.com; long-term charts can be obtained from the Securities Research Company at www.srcstockcharts.com. Both are pricey, alas, so once again, try your library first.

> **Red Flags**
>
> Be sure any long-term charts you consult use logarithmic scaling, not standard scaling! Log scaling uses percentage changes in price—not dollar changes—as the unit of measure on the Y axis. That makes sense, because any given change in dollar amount has more impact when a stock is cheap, less when it's expensive.

Finding Stocks to Research

Now you've got your database, a hat full of a million rabbits. How do you go about deciding which rabbit to pull out for a closer look? Remember, it takes a lot of time to investigate even one company, and you won't always decide to buy after you do all that research. So it pays to choose candidates carefully.

It turns out there are three ways to go about it: (1) look into businesses or industries with which you're already familiar; (2) sift stocks through various criteria you set up; (3) read to get ideas. And of course, you can do all three.

Look at Businesses You Already Know Something About

This is a favorite of Peter Lynch, the former Magellan Fund money manager, and particularly relevant for growth-oriented investors. The notion is that during your everyday life as a consumer, worker, or even idle observer, you may find that there's a particular industry or even a company that you're quite familiar with, and that this familiarity could give you an edge over Wall Street analysts and money managers.

Maybe you've found a new chain store to shop at that you never heard of, and you're impressed with its customer service and product line. Maybe you work inside a given industry, and have some hunches about upcoming trends that Wall Street won't be picking up on for some time.

This approach may give you some companies to look at, but bear in mind they're still only candidates. Don't be too eager to snap them up just because of your supposed insider knowledge. You'll still have to do a lot of skeptical reading and thinking before you can decide whether you've got a winner.

Red Flags

One potential danger in investing in what you know is underdiversification. If you're a doctor, for example, you may know something about pharmaceutical or medical supply companies, but you'll have to mull over whether you feel comfortable confining your stock picks to just those companies. Your job and their fortunes might be too closely tied together. If you're well diversified elsewhere in your portfolio, the increased risk may be reasonable compared to the chance to use your expertise, but a pink slip in the office and red ink in your portfolio make a disastrous combination.

Sift and Screen

You can also narrow the field by setting up criteria that stocks must meet:

You might find you need more diversification based on the stocks you already own. For example, if most of your holdings are small cap stocks, you might decide that your next purchase should be a large cap company. That would give you a direction for further searching by another method.

A more complicated method is to screen stocks for desirable characteristics. Essentially, you use software to include or exclude companies based on size, P/E and other valuation ratios, and a slew of other ratios and financials. Screening tools are available from many sources; for example, a premium subscription to Morningstar.com.

Professional money managers do a lot of screening, but that's because they need to own a lot of stocks. But you don't—after all, you've got a mutual fund for diversification. So for you, screening may be overkill. What you really need as a part-time stock picker is just a few good ideas.

To screen, you use a software tool to comb a database for stocks that meet certain characteristics: low P/E, high dividend yield, accelerating earnings growth, or pretty much any measure or combination of measures you want.

Exactly what you can search for depends on the particular software package, but they're all pretty similar. For example, you can tell the software to find all companies with a P/E of more than 40, or all companies in the media sector. You can combine as many criteria as you like before clicking the Search button.

You can make up a screen of your own, or you can use canned screens already set up by the database vendor. For example, Morningstar's premium service provides screens that purport to identify "Wealth Creators" or "Bargain Stocks."

Not only are canned screens convenient, but you can learn from them what the screen designer felt was important. But be aware that even the fanciest screens will catch some bad companies along with the good. They're only a starting point for further investigation.

 The Bottom Line

You can try the basic screener at Morningstar.com for free; another free screener is available at Yahoo.com. If you really get into it, though, go for the professional-quality MSN Money Investment Toolbox. It's also free (though it requires Internet Explorer and a Microsoft .NET passport). You can find it at www. moneycentral.msn.com/investor/controls/ finderpro.asp.

Read for Ideas

Even though I'm not running a big mutual fund anymore, I still like to read what industry professionals are doing, just to get their ideas. Here are some of my favorites:

Barron's. Standard Sunday reading for money managers. Pros feel it's an honor to appear in *Barron's*, so it gets interviews from the cream of the crop. It's a good way to pick up a lot of relatively unfiltered observations and advice.

The Wall Street Transcript. More interviews with pros, and even less-filtered than *Barron's*. But it's pricey, so get it at your library if you can.

Investext. Electronic delivery of Wall Street research reports written by analysts at a variety of investment banks, brokerages, and consulting firms. It, too, may be available at your library, but don't fret if you can't get it.

Who should you pay attention to in all this reading? Market strategists are the most fun—their interest in the big picture makes for the best cocktail-party conversation. But you'll get more actionable tips from portfolio managers working in the trenches. And the shrewdest ideas of all tend to come from industry analysts, because they spend their time looking hard at a relative handful of stocks.

What about conflicts of interest? Can you really trust any of these guys? The fact is, SEC scrutiny has made money managers very careful about what they say in print. Beyond that, if a successful manager is talking up a stock that he owns, it's because he wants it to go up. You want the stocks you own to go up, too, so the two of you have the same goal.

The real thing to be careful about is how fresh or stale an interview is. If it's two weeks old or more, you need to check the stock price to see if it's gone up significantly since then.

And of course it goes without saying that regardless of how hard a manager or analyst touts a stock, you're still going to do your own research before deciding whether to buy. If the manager is popular with investors, you may have to do that research quickly, but you'll still do it. It's better to miss a short-term run-up in price than to make a long-term mistake.

The Bottom Line

Studies suggest that in general, good industry analysts add more value to stock-picking than do fund managers. This, in part, has to do with focus. Money managers must look at stocks in all sectors and industries, but analysts typically cover just a few industries. A narrower focus means more time spent applying consistent methods for selection and valuation, resulting in a higher percentage of winners.

Who Not to Listen To

There are countless newsletters advocating sure-fire investing styles, or touting one stock after another as can't-miss winners. Should you be reading them, too? My recommendation is no, especially when you're starting out.

Newsletters in general aren't very highly regarded among investment professionals, and there's a good reason why: anyone can write one and say nearly anything. Even a convicted felon who wouldn't be able to register with the SEC as an investment advisor can write one!

Plus, newsletter authors are under the compulsion to continually come up with something new to say—such as a new list of wonder stocks each week. The effect may be to persuade you to trade more often than you should. As you'll see in Chapter 10, that's one of the worst mistakes you can make.

How about chat rooms and message boards on the Internet, where participants can exchange stock tips? Despite their popularity, and despite their sponsorship by seemingly legit outfits, I don't like them. In my opinion, they're even worse than newsletters. You often have no clue whom you're dealing with or what their credentials are, if any. And just as with newsletters, exposing yourself to lots of feverish stock ideas may tempt you to trade more than you should.

Investigating a Specific Stock

Suppose you've found a company that looks promising. It's time to do some concentrated research.

Visit the company website to collect annual reports, investor presentations, and more. We look at this in more detail in the next section.

Do lots of targeted reading about the company and its industry. You should be able to pick up some trends just from your general reading; if you have time, you can also read industry trade magazines. Your librarian may be able to help you look these up. Some magazines now have websites in addition to their printed versions. You're looking for trends that affect the entire industry, as well as any direct mention of the company or its competitors.

Review the market sentiment—that is, what analysts are saying about the company. Aside from your broad-based database, check the *Wall Street Journal*, *Barron's*, and the other publications previously mentioned.

Utilize personal sources. If you know someone who works in the industry, give that person a call and see what he or she has to say. However, don't call if the person actually works for the company in question! It could be considered insider information by the SEC.

You'll also be assessing whether this stock fits your preferred investing style—generally leaning toward either growth or value—and whether the market is valuing the stock correctly. But I'm going to save that for Chapter 8, because it's as much about analysis as it is about pure research.

What to Look For at the Company Website

Your first stop in gathering detailed information about a company will always be the company itself. Ten years ago, this would have meant calling up the company's investor relations department and asking for information to be mailed to you. Today, it's usually quicker to visit the company website.

For example, if you want to learn more about Johnson & Johnson, you go to their website at www.jnj.com, click Investor Relations, and see the following links. They're typical of what you should expect from nearly any company:

Stock information. This includes price, dividends, splits, and so on.

Shareholder services. Here you can learn whether a company offers a dividend reinvestment plan, or DRIP.

SEC filings. Most important is the 10-K, or annual filing, with its detailed financial statements about the company, including balance sheets, income statements, and statements of cash flows. Much of this information can also be found in the company's annual report, but because the 10-K doesn't have a bunch of fancy photos and graphics, it's usually quicker to download it. You can also get 10-Qs, which are the quarterly versions of the same information.

Proxy. The proxy spells out issues being submitted to a vote by shareholders. More important, the proxy contains information about the board of directors and executive compensation, helping you size up management's integrity.

Financial information. The company helpfully provides estimates of where earnings per share are headed for the remainder of this year or for next year, as provided by Wall Street analysts. These are important because they help you understand what most people are expecting from the company. Johnson & Johnson gets them from a service called First Call; other services that provide earnings estimates include Zacks and I/B/E/S. Most companies don't make it so easy to find this information, but you'll also find Wall Street estimates in your general-purpose database, such as Value Line or Morningstar.

Company information. Aside from a brief description of the company and a link to information about strategic planning, Johnson & Johnson also uses this page to state its policy on SEC *Regulation F.D.*—for example, who is authorized to speak to investors on behalf of the company.

> (S) **Market Speak** _____
>
> **Regulation F.D.** was enacted by the SEC in 1999 to ensure that small investors get the same access to company information as big institutional investors. Not only are you protected against a company leaking important information only to the big guys, but you also get to listen to webcasts and other presentations at which analysts ask questions of management. This is a great way to learn about current issues with the company.

Webcasts/Presentations. Thanks to Regulation F.D. and the Internet, you can listen in on presentations made by J&J management to big institutional investors on a variety of subjects. And you can sign up for quarterly earnings conference calls, where analysts quiz J&J management on whatever issues they think are important. This can be especially useful in the early stages of your research.

News releases. Standard fare, but worth scanning for announcements of new products or services, management changes, and so on. Many companies allow you to sign up for e-mail news updates.

Other information. At the J&J site this is a grab-bag of information, including details on drugs in research and development, detailed information on the board of directors, various FAQs, and an interface for requesting documents.

If you happen to be researching a tiny, obscure company that doesn't maintain a good website, you can go to other places to get much of this information. For example, 10-Ks are available on the web through an SEC service called EDGAR, at www. sec.gov/edgar.shtml. When you're first starting out, though, I recommend sticking with companies that make it easy for you. After all, there are loads of them out there, and some are great investments.

You may be thinking that all this information gathering is just scratching the surface. If so, you're right. It's essentially to gather facts and expert opinions, of course, but you still have to sift through them yourself, summarize what you know and don't know, and then make up your own mind about who's right, who's wrong, and what's missing. That's what the next chapter is all about.

The Least You Need to Know

- ◆ It's essential to keep up on general business and economic news, through newspapers such as *The Wall Street Journal* and magazines such as *Forbes*.

- ◆ You can find interesting stocks three ways: following up on ideas you observe from everyday life, screening stocks through specific criteria, and doing lots of reading.

- ◆ You can also get stock ideas by reading stock-specific publications such as *Barron's*, TheStreet.Com, or *Investors Business Daily*.

- For snapshot summaries of stocks and companies, either check your library for Value Line, or subscribe to an online database such as Morningstar's.

- Digging into a specific stock and company requires research with multiple sources, plus a visit to the company website for its 10-K, annual report, and investor presentations.

8

When to Buy

In This Chapter

- ◆ Gauging market sentiment
- ◆ Finding an edge—is the market wrong?
- ◆ Making your case
- ◆ Two buy examples
- ◆ Staying on the case

You've found an absolutely captivating stock, done your initial research, and so far you like what you see. You don't want to risk missing this opportunity, so is it time to call your broker or visit your online account and buy some shares?

Not quite. That would be hasty and emotional, and haste and emotion are two things that successful investors avoid.

First, you've got to define what type of stock it is, and whether it fits into your investing style. After that, you've got to determine what the market thinks, and why. And last and most important, you've got to decide whether the market's assumptions are right or wrong. That's where you find opportunity, if it's there to be found.

If it's a value stock, are investors right in pricing it down there with the dust balls at the bottom of the cellar—or are they focusing too hard on temporary bad news, even as the fundamentals have gotten stronger? If it's a growth stock that has begun to waver, is the market right in thinking it's overvalued? Or does your analysis of the business show there's room for yet more growth?

Or wonder of wonders, have you stumbled across that rare creature, a growth stock masquerading as a value stock, perhaps because the industry is one that most investors find boring?

This chapter takes you through this process step by step, building what's known as a *buy case*. We talk about the positives that signal a great buy case, and the negatives that signal a bad one. This chapter even walks you through a couple of actual buy cases I developed while writing this book. Finally, we wrap up with a look at how to monitor your stocks after you've bought them.

What's the Valuation?

One of the first things you look at is known as valuation—that is, the value placed on the stock and the underlying business. You want to know this because, as a long-term investor, you're only interested in buying stocks at a discount compared to the value of the business. That way, the most likely direction for the stock price to go is up.

You also need to know the valuation in order to start thinking about whether the stock leans toward either value or growth, meaning it does or doesn't fit your investing style. We talk more about this shortly.

There are two very different approaches to valuation. The first is to calculate the relative valuation—that is, the value investors are placing on this stock compared to stocks in general, or compared to other stocks in the same industry. That's the approach I recommend you use, as long as you observe a few caveats and qualifications.

The second approach is to calculate the intrinsic value of the underlying business, disregarding the price of the stock. It's a much harder calculation, full of pitfalls. We look at it briefly, but it's not something I recommend you try at home.

Relative Valuation Using Multiples

What are multiples? Actually, it's just a fancy Wall Street term for financial ratios, such as price to earnings, price to book value, and so on. So multiples-based valuation is just valuation using one or more of these ratios.

For example, with P/E, the most telling measure is to compare the P/E of the stock to the average P/E for all stocks. That tells you what price investors are willing to pay for the stock's earnings, versus the price they're willing to pay on average for a stock.

The Bottom Line

Analysts and investors sometimes speak of price to earnings (P/E) as a multiple rather than a ratio. The reasoning is this: Given earnings of x dollars for the current quarter, how many times that amount would investors be willing to pay for the stock? Do you multiply by 15? By 20? If so, you've got a P/E multiple of 15, or 20, or what have you.

Next on the list, you can compare the current P/E of the stock to its historical P/Es, seeing what investors are willing to pay for earnings now versus at various times in the past. This can give you a picture of how the stock has moved up and down in investors' estimation of its value over time.

Last in importance, but still useful, you can compare the P/E of the stock to the average P/E for all stocks in its sector or industry.

Valuation is especially helpful when screening for value stocks—stocks priced unusually low for the value of the underlying business. (If you remember, we discussed screening back in Chapter 7.) If a stock is in the bottom 10 or 20 percent of the market for P/E, for example, you know you're most likely looking at a potential value stock, other things being equal.

The Bottom Line

Remember that with price to earnings, the price is always the current price, but the earnings may be actual or projected. If it's early in the company's fiscal year, you want to look at projected earnings for the full year, which may include some actual earnings for the start of the year and an estimate for the balance. If it's toward the end of the fiscal year, on the other hand, you want to look at analysts' estimates of earnings for next year.

Useful Multiples to Look At

Here are the most-useful multiples for valuation, along with tips on when they're appropriate. You can find these for any stock or sector, as well as for the market overall, in any good stocks database. (If you need to refresh your memory about databases, look back at Chapter 7.)

Price to earnings, or P/E. The single most important measure when considering valuation. Note that above-average growth usually means a higher P/E, whereas above-average risk usually means a lower P/E—investors like to pay for growth, but they don't like to pay for what they see as risk. You need to be careful about P/E, however, because accounting issues can play havoc with the quality of earnings. For example, if a company recently sold off a business, this may have artificially inflated earnings for that period—meaning you need to factor out the sale to arrive at a truer measure of P/E.

Price to book, or P/B. The "book" here means inventory or physical plant—in other words, the value of assets "on the books." Least useful for service companies, or companies whose primary assets are intellectual property, such as software companies. Most useful for energy, commodities, and financial services companies.

Price to cash flow, or P/CF. Cash flow represents cash that actually changes hands, as opposed to earnings, which can include things such as sales not yet paid for, as well as depreciation, an accounting charge that companies record every year to reflect the declining value of things such as equipment. P/CF is often used when valuing companies with lots of tangible assets, such as real estate, car makers, cable television providers, or commodities such as oil or gold.

Price to sales, or P/S. Price divided by sales per share. Like P/CF, it may be cleaner in some cases than P/E, because some accounting tricks are screened out. Plus, it's not as volatile from year to year as P/E; this makes it handy for companies in cyclical industries, such as car makers.

Dividend yield. Annual dividends divided by the stock price—in other words, the percentage of your purchase price that's returned to you in dividends every year. Lower stock prices tend to produce higher dividend yields, pointing toward possible value buys. But you've got to do a lot of homework here; for starters, not all stocks pay dividends.

So which of these should you look at for a stock? All of them, both to get a full picture and to make sure there are no inconsistencies. If you do find a multiple that doesn't jibe with the others, it might be a sign the company is trying to hide something. For example, if relative P/E is much lower than relative P/CF, the company may be boosting accruals (such as sales not yet paid for) to make its earnings look better than they are.

> **Red Flags**
>
> One multiple I recommend you don't use is P/E to growth, or PEG. Why? Well, it's difficult to forecast growth. And if that weren't enough, the relationship between P/E and growth isn't linear anyway! That makes PEG a very hard number to interpret. Many growth fund managers like PEG, but they've got a lot of practice reading tea leaves and casting the I Ching, and you don't—at least not yet.

Intrinsic Value

The other approach to valuation is to try and calculate the "intrinsic value" of the business, arriving at a hard number that's independent of the stock price.

The original standard for this is something called the dividend discount model, as expounded by John Burr Williams in his 1938 book *The Theory of Investment Value*. Subsequently, other models have been developed that are even more complex. All the models try to arrive at a value for the future cash flow from a business, adjusting for the fact that a dollar today is worth more than the promise of a dollar tomorrow.

The idea is that your valuation will be gloriously independent of the market, but these methods never quite deliver. They still reflect market valuations, usually through their choice of discount rate (essentially the interest rate); they require lots of estimates and assumptions, many of which are quite difficult to arrive at; and small differences in inputs to the equations can result in big differences in the final number.

For me, and for many other professional investors, multiples-based valuation is the better way to go, being simpler and less prone to manipulation. If you do run across an analyst who's using an intrinsic value model to arrive at a valuation, your best defense is to check the analyst's assumptions. That will give you some idea of whether the end result can be trusted.

Figuring Out What You Think Versus What the Market Thinks

With the stock's valuation in hand, you can begin to draw together the information you've gathered, aiming for a meaningful whole. This includes where the stock might fit in your portfolio; what analysts and pundits are saying; your own knowledge of the company and industry; and, most crucially, whether you think the assumptions being made by other investors are right or wrong.

Remember, the average opinion of investors can be thought of as being summarized by the valuation. What you want to analyze are the most-cited positives and negatives, because they represent the rationales behind the valuation. You can learn these by reading the opinions of analysts, portfolio managers, and pundits as expressed in news stories. In addition, most analysts' reports will include a discussion of key issues identified as such.

I find it helpful to look separately at both the positives and negatives for a stock—which is one reason I like Morningstar's handy summaries of "Bulls Say" versus "Bears Say." If you want to make a case to buy a stock, you need to find reasons why the bears are wrong, or why the bulls aren't bullish enough. At the same time, you've also got to try and be more bearish than the bears, racking your brains for any negatives they might have missed. Such independent analysis is helpful for judging when it's time to sell, too.

The Bottom Line

Here's an example of spotting a negative ahead of the crowd. Back when I was still running my mutual funds, I learned that a certain utility with a nuclear plant was having regulatory problems. I didn't happen to own that stock, but I did own a bunch of other utility stocks with nuclear plants.

Were the bears (or anyone else) talking about this regulatory problem as an issue for nuclear plants in general? Nope; not a peep. But I went ahead and sold, figuring the market would soon get nervous about all nuclear plants. In fact, the market did catch on, and the stocks later declined.

Ethical Concerns and Portfolio Fit

As mentioned in Chapter 6, many individuals have begun practicing socially responsible investing. If you're one of them, now is a good time to weigh any potential deal breakers you've come across during your investigation of the company or industry.

It's also a good time to look at this stock in the context of your portfolio: Does it decrease or increase your overall diversification? If it decreases diversification, are you comfortable with the added risk?

Stock Versus Style

Basically, is it a growth stock or a value stock, and are you a growth investor or a value investor? The point of sticking mostly to growth or to value (especially in the beginning) is that it forces you to think in a disciplined manner. By comparing each stock you look at to the ground rules for your style, you'll develop your skills within a meaningful context, rather than at random.

Having to honor an investing style is like learning to write good poems. Anyone can write free verse, but you learn more by struggling with rhyme.

Analyzing the Assumptions Behind a Value Stock

Typically, a stock is considered a value stock because it has a low valuation, and it has a low valuation because of neutral to negative perceptions on the part of the market. For example, the business may have had some well-publicized bad news, or the industry as a whole may be a cyclical one that's in the dumps at the moment. Or the company simply may be too small or obscure (or bland) to have gotten much notice so far.

The key here is that low valuations by themselves aren't enough to make a value stock a buy. Again, you need to be able to make the case that the market has either overstated the negatives or failed to see a big positive. In effect, you need to be able to say that the business is a good one or is going to be a good one, better than the market realizes. I'll walk you through how to do this shortly, in an example buy case.

Analyzing the Assumptions Behind a Growth Stock

As already noted, many growth stocks will already have relatively high valuations, because the market has already built reports of revenue or earnings growth in to the share price.

If you're going to get on board, too, you have to make the case that growth will continue for some time to come, rather than stall. Because the price is already relatively high, and because the future is hard to predict, there's a greater danger than with a value stock of not getting a bargain. So you've got to decide whether bullish analysts are overly optimistic or on target, even as you consider whether bearish analysts have caught all the potential negatives.

In rare cases you may be able to spot a growth stock before the market has caught on. In fact, this is Peter Lynch's preferred approach to stock hunting. Lynch wasn't just a growth investor, though; he thought in terms of both growth and value. Many of the picks described in his books were stocks that had fallen out of favor but then rebounded, in effect turning into growth stocks during the time he owned them.

Keep in mind that there are only a few ways a company can keep growing earnings of its existing businesses: (1) selling more, which could involve expanding into new markets or adding new products and services; (2) raising prices; or (3) cutting costs. Companies are always peddling stories to investors about how they plan to grow or keep growing. Whatever the story, it should fit into one of these three scenarios, and it should be plausible.

Be wary of plans to grow earnings through financial manipulation: buying an operation, selling one, or taking on more debt. These can work short-term, but rarely result in long-term gains.

Stating Your Buy Case

Let's suppose that after all this work, you still like what you see. Go ahead and write down your buy case—the reasons you believe you should buy the stock. Here's what to summarize in your buy case:

- The company's business.
- The most important business trend you've spotted.
- The most important external factors, whether economic, demographic, technological, environmental, or what have you.
- The market's valuation, and the rationale behind it.
- What the market has missed that you've picked up on.

A good buy case is easy to understand. If you can't explain the company's business in a few sentences, you shouldn't own the stock. How did I avoid getting caught in the WorldCom disaster? I couldn't explain how telecommunications reselling could generate fabulous profits!

A buy case should also be reasonable. This is especially important for growth stocks. Try this as a test: if growth meets your expectations, how big will the company be in five years, and is that reasonable? For example, suppose you expect a company with $10 billion in current sales to grow 40 percent a year for the next 5 years. That means that in 5 years, sales will be $40 billion. Is that reasonable, given the overall size of the market for the industry in question?

A buy case should also give you a reason to buy now. This is particularly important for value stocks. Cheap stocks can stay cheap a very long time, in which case we call them value traps, not value stocks. You want to identify a catalyst that leads to recognition of that value in your lifetime—for example, a new or revamped product or service.

A very good buy case gives you more than one way to win—for example, sales could increase, or the company could be acquired. An extra way to win is doubly important if your buy case is based partly on an external factor, such as the economy picking up. Even if the economy doesn't pick up, you may still come out ahead if your other way to win pans out.

Example: A Buy Case for Old Army

For example, suppose you recently went to your local Old Army store (the company is hypothetical) and found that you bought much more than you expected to. This turns you on to the stock as a possibility, and you begin researching. Eventually you put together a buy case as follows:

- Old Army is a clothing store providing "the basics" through a chain of stores in the Midwest.

- Based on personal experience, your reading, and a visit to the company website, it's clear that Old Army is adapting to an aging population. The company has revamped its clothing line so that it appeals to a broad range of consumers, not just the teen crowd. Analysts believe that sales should improve, and so do you. In fact, you're a little more bullish than some of the bullish analysts.

- A look at your stock database reveals that Old Army's stock is trading at a significant discount compared to both the retail clothing industry and the S&P 500. Its price to earnings is only ⅔ of the industry P/E, and its price to book is ½ of the industry P/B, and the industry as a whole is cheaper than the market.

- Your reading has alerted you to a slew of recent acquisitions in the retail industry. More than that, your analysis of Old Army as a relatively small company in an industry of behemoths, with a strong free cash flow, leads you to conclude that Old Army is an attractive takeover candidate at its current stock price. Wow!

The Bottom Line

To the beginning investor, it may seem that a piece of analysis such as figuring out that Old Army is a potential takeover canddate requires more business and financial acumen than you can ever hope to acquire. You've got to be able to interpret a company's annual report, synthesize snips and fragments of industry news, and put it all together to reach a conclusion that may not have been reported anywhere in your reading.

But take heart. Skill in investing is largely a matter of experience. Detail by detail, with each success, each mistake, you build a mosaic of expertise. Depending on how much time you put into it, you'll start having "Aha!" moments as particular pieces of that mosaic click into place. That's when investing really becomes fun.

You finish your buy case for Old Army by dating it and filing it in your Old Army file folder. You're going to save the buy case for as long as you own the stock. And if in the interim you change your thinking about Old Army, you're going to write a new buy case, date it, and save it along with the old one.

Why hang on to all this information? Because, even though we're calling them buy cases, they'll be just as important when you start thinking about selling. You don't just make a decision to own a stock on the day you buy it. You make that choice every day you continue to own it.

Positives to Look For

There are some specific good things to look for when formulating a buy case, including the following:

Positive #1: Improving earnings estimates, as reported in news about the company. Even better is a positive earnings surprise, when earnings turn out to be much better than analysts expected. This can appear in news about the company (*Barron's* in particular carries a weekly list of earnings surprises), or in analysts' reports when quarterly earnings are released.

Positive #2: News of a new product that's expected to do well in the marketplace.

Positive #3: Recent changes in legislation or regulation that are likely to benefit the company. Such changes are infrequent, but can be powerful. For example, federal tax legislation promoting IRAs and 401(k)s in the early 1980s gave a huge boost to companies in the money management business, such as T. Rowe Price.

Note that these first three items all believe the ancient Wall Street wisdom of "Buy on the rumor, sell on the news." In fact, you'll usually have plenty of time to buy on the news, given that it generally takes a while for positive developments to impact price. As long as you're reasonably early in the cycle, you don't have to be first in line. Continuing …

Positive #4: Insider buying. New stock purchases by top management are always a good sign. Again, you'll find such information in news articles and analysts' reports.

Positive #5: Low valuations. See the discussion of valuation earlier in this chapter (refer to the "What's the Valuation?" section).

Positive #6: A commodity where supply is shrinking and demand increasing. Your best sources for this are industry analysts. A great current example is oil. The price has gone up because demand is rising as the world economy rebounds and emerging markets develop—even as it's getting harder and harder to find new reserves.

Background Positives

There are some positives about a company that may not be as noticeable, but are still good signs. I call these background positives. They include …

Economic and demographic trends that help the company. You'll get these from your general business reading. Market strategists in particular like to talk about this sort of thing. You may also find yourself reading about a trend, then thinking about what sort of businesses would benefit from it.

Or you may notice friends, family, or co-workers changing their habits, and decide to pay attention to articles that talk about such changes.

Good company management. This doesn't mean the CEO is a media darling, looks good on webcasts, and answers questions with an air of authority. In fact, that kind of charisma might be a bad sign, the hallmark of an imperial CEO! No, I'm talking about good management, which consists of things such as the following:

+ Management owns a sizeable amount of company stock.

+ A reasonable long-term strategy, with some measurable targets to flesh out the rhetoric. A good example is General Electric's strategy, available on its website. The section titled "Leadership and Metrics" cites highly specific goals, such as "8 percent organic revenue growth and 10 percent+ earnings growth, with operating cash flow growth greater than earnings."

+ Managers give clear and reasonable answers to questions during webcasts and other presentations.

+ Managers don't just tout successes, but freely discuss risks and problems, too.

+ The CEO doesn't have a second part-time job at another company's board or as head of a trade organization; the board members are clearly qualified and have no ties to the company (aside from a few management representatives). What you're looking for here is an absence of negatives; the place to look is the proxy statement, as discussed in Chapter 7.

♦ Executive compensation is reasonable, given performance. Again, check the proxy. From your general reading, you'll know a problem when you see it. As an example of the absence of a problem, Steve Ballmer and Bill Gates at Microsoft took less than $600,000 in salary in fiscal 2004.

There you have the positives ... and now for the negatives.

Warning Signs

Here are some things to watch out for:

Negative #1: Increasing competition. This won't go away, no matter what management tells you. For example, it wasn't hard a few years ago to see why business was going to be tough for Eastman Kodak—digital photography was winning, even if Kodak couldn't admit it.

Negative #2: Pending litigation or harmful legislation, especially when the suit comes to trial or the bill is about to be passed. Never stake your money on a successful outcome in court. Texaco investors can tell you all about that, because the company went into bankruptcy after losing a court case to Pennzoil. Pending suits and legislation are generally written about by analysts if they're important.

Negative #3: Plans to "shrink to growth." That's my phrase for announcements by companies whose products or services are under attack that they're going to cut costs as a way of resuming growth. Eastman Kodak is again a good example of the futility of such attempts. For all its restructuring, the company is still having trouble transforming itself into a competitor again.

Negative #4: Too much debt. How much is too much varies by industry. For example, financial companies always carry a lot of debt as part of doing business; whereas if an industrial company has a debt-to-equity ratio of more than 1.00, it's time to pay attention. The company may not be able to meet its obligations during an economic downturn. Again, if debt is a problem, analysts will be writing about it.

Negative #5: The company trades close to the value of the cash on its balance sheet. In other words, cash minus debt is close to the market cap. This may happen if the company raised a lot of cash during its initial public offering, but since then hasn't managed to make any money on its alleged product or service. In such a case, investors are already aware the company is a zombie, and that all that cash is going to be spent doing nothing until there's no cash left to spend. Good examples of this are some of the dot.com companies that went broke.

Negative #6: New corporate headquarters. This is a favorite of mine. Not infallible, but a fancy new headquarters is often a canary-in-the-mineshaft warning of growing corporate hubris. This would have been a good indicator for Enron, which was in the middle of building a gleaming new building around the time everything collapsed.

Building Into Positions

We discussed the mechanics of entering your buy order in Chapter 4; review if necessary.

Beyond that, I'm a big believer in averaging into positions. In other words, if the total number of shares you want to buy is at all sizeable—say, more than 50 shares or shares with a total cost above $2,000—don't buy it all at once. Instead, buy one half now, one half in a month.

Why do it this way? Because you can't time the market. If you buy it all now and the stock dips a little next week, you may kick yourself (though you shouldn't) for not having waited to get a better deal. By averaging into positions, you avoid second-guessing yourself.

However, if your position is a small one, there's no point in making several buys. Your trading costs would be too high in comparison with the number of shares.

Two Buy Case Examples

Here are two actual buy cases I put together on July 15, 2005, as I was writing this book. Bear in mind that although I bought these stocks myself, these are examples, not recommendations. By the time you read this, the picture for both stocks will almost certainly have changed.

In both cases, I got most of the financial data from Morningstar's premium subscription service. Other information came from reading analysts' reports, visiting the company websites, and lots of general reading.

Value Buy: Pfizer at $28

I got interested in this company by thinking about industries that were in the dog house. Also, this stock in particular was recommended by some value managers in interviews. (I looked at Merck, too, but litigation over that company's COX-2 painkiller, Vioxx, looked like it would be unusually troublesome.)

My main reason for buying Pfizer was its valuation. It was trading at 13 times next year's earnings, well below the market and significantly below the stock's historical valuations. Plus it had a 2.6 percent dividend yield, above the market average.

The stock was down for all the very well-publicized reasons: safety issues with the COX-2 pain medications Bextra and Celebrex, plus negative press about pharmaceutical pricing and marketing. In addition, several drugs would soon be losing patent protection. Once a growth stock, now a value stock; so the world goes round.

Even so, as a company Pfizer had incredible resources. Financially it was very strong, with a

AAA *credit rating* and lots of cash. That means it could continue to maintain a massive R&D effort, while also outright buying new drugs to market. All together, I felt it was an opportunity to buy a high-quality company at an unusually low price. The company was still very profitable, and they'd instituted a cost-cutting effort that was expected to boost 2006 earnings.

> **$ Market Speak**
>
> **Credit ratings** are a quick way of assessing the financial health of a corporation. They're issued by credit rating agencies—Moody's and Standard & Poor's are the best known—based on their evaluation of the company's current position and prospects. As in your high school report card, an "A" rating indicates top performance, with "AAA" forming the honor society. Companies with B ratings are pretty average, those with "C's" are barely passing, and companies earning a "D" are in default, which is a polite term for bankruptcy.

The only negative: transparency wasn't particularly high. Lots of acquisitions made it a bit tougher to read the balance sheet. And the company didn't keep an archive of presentations on its website, making it harder to research what investors had already been told. On the other hand, Pfizer was improving their governance practices. They'd instituted annual elections for directors, giving shareholders the power to vote out bad directors.

I consider this a prototypical value recommendation. The negatives are very visible, but the stock price more than compensates. You can also see that very few real-world buys will meet all your criteria. I'd like this buy case better if the specter of additional regulation or legislation wasn't hanging over the industry as a whole—but in that case, the stock wouldn't be so cheap.

Looking forward, I'd expect to see improved earnings in 2006, even as I'd expect the stock's P/E to increase slightly above that for the market as a whole, in recognition of the company's continued profitability.

Growth Buy: Microsoft at $26

This buy came partly from the realization that I hadn't upgraded the software on my computer for some time—I was still using Windows XP and Office 2003. And both Windows and Office are scheduled for an upgrade in 2006. This is good news for a company with a near monopoly in both operating systems and productivity software.

I also liked Microsoft because it wasn't particularly expensive for such a high-quality growth company. It was selling for roughly 20 times next year's earnings, with a 1.2 percent dividend yield. (I know, I'm betraying my roots as a value investor.)

Like Pfizer, Microsoft had an incredibly strong balance sheet with lots of cash, giving the company lots of room to grow dividends. Plus they had extremely good corporate governance practices: they'd stopped issuing stock options, and they made tons of information available to investors on their website.

The risk, of course, was that Microsoft might lose its monopoly. But I wasn't as concerned as I might have been a year ago. The threat of antitrust lawsuits has faded, and open-source software didn't appear to be much competition in the immediate future.

The company had worldwide exposure, meaning it could benefit from growth elsewhere in the world, especially in emerging markets. (A China play!) Although piracy has been an issue in such markets, I suspected this was likely to diminish, given better controls over software duplication and trade agreements.

For the future, my buy case predicted continued growth in earnings, plus either growth in dividends or the announcement of stock buy-backs by the company.

Monitoring Your Buy Case

After you've bought your stock, how much attention should you pay to it? Should you have CNBC on at all times at work or at home, so you can monitor every fluctuation in the market?

Of course not. But how much time should you spend on the stocks you own, and what should that time consist of?

I recommend you spend quality time with your stocks, not quantity time. That means reviewing your stock portfolio on a regular basis, comparing the current condition of your stocks to your original buy cases.

Maybe it's a Saturday-morning project or maybe it's Wednesday night. Just take the time to review the news about your stocks and their industries. Check price movements, and look at your buy case to see if it still holds water.

I also recommend you keep a log of the time you spend on your stocks, and file it in the same drawer where you file your buy cases. You can put notes and thoughts into the log, or just use it to track the hours you put in. It's a good way to reinforce staying on top of things rather than letting them slide.

The Least You Need to Know

- Knowing a stock's valuation lets you weigh what investors think of that stock versus its historic performance, other stocks in that industry, and the market overall.
- Good measures for relative valuation are P/E, P/B, P/S, and dividend yield.
- Value investors look for stocks that typically have low valuations; growth investors typically look at stocks with higher valuations as well as recent growth in earnings and revenue.

- After you've analyzed a stock and find you still like it, write down a concise but clear case that encapsulates the data and your reasoning.

- After buying a stock, you should spend some quality time with it each week, reviewing news and prices and checking whether your buy case is still valid.

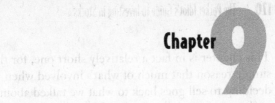

Chapter 9

When to Sell

In This Chapter

- Selling based on facts, not feelings
- All bad news isn't alike
- Selling for diversification
- Tax planning

If the decision of when and what to buy is important, the decision of when to sell is just as much so—and presents an equal chance to make mistakes.

Unskilled investors tend not only to buy at the wrong times, but to sell at the wrong times—either too soon or, much worse, too late. They sell a winner out of fear that some unstated law of nature dictates it can't go higher, or hang on to a loser with a death grip, praying it will somehow revive.

You don't want to be like that. You want logic and research to dictate when you sell, not emotion and superstition. Fortunately, it's not as hard as it might seem.

This chapter is in fact a relatively short one, for the simple reason that much of what's involved when deciding to sell goes back to what we talked about in the previous chapter—your buy case. If you've made a good buy case, you've got the foundation for deciding when to sell.

When Not To Sell

As we talk about shortly, the most common reason to sell is when something has happened to flip your buy case from positive to negative. That leaves a host of fraudulent reasons to sell—signals you should ignore, because they're not really signals, but noise.

The price has dropped. If your buy case remains strong, you could well be better off buying more rather than selling. A good tip to avoid panicking over short-term price moves is to remember to monitor companies, not stocks. Don't check the stock price 20 times a day. Instead, spend quality time each week reading the industry news, checking in with analysts' reports, and looking at the fundamentals. Also make sure you look at your stock relative to the market. If all stocks have gone down, it's not a problem with yours.

The price has gone up. As mentioned before, we tend to think of common sense as a substitute for logic. Common sense suggests that if a stock price has gone up, it's bound to come down, like tossing an apple in the air. This is fallacious. Although no one can predict the market in the short term, a stock price that's gone up today is no more fated to come down tomorrow than a penny that's landed heads on one toss is fated to land tails on the next. You're not buying and selling on short-term ups and downs anyway. So don't act on common sense; stick to your buy case.

Someone cries "Wolf." Because investing always seems to have its mysterious aspects, you may be tempted at one time or another to sell because of something you've heard but don't understand. For example:

♦ As you and your buddy stand in line at Starbuck's, he mentions he's heard a rumor of problems with your stock. He's unable to provide a source, but insists it was a real rumor.

♦ A talking head on CNBC outlines a sell case for your stock. You don't know who he is, and he's not saying anything new—you've already discounted these negatives—but still, he makes you nervous.

♦ You scan a headline that the company's latest quarterly earnings are disappointing, but in your chagrin, fail to read the body of the article. If you had, you'd have learned that both management and analysts are making positive noises about improvements in earnings for the remainder of the year.

You can stop such scares in their tracks by relying on your usual research methods any time you hear something puzzling or strange. Is there in fact some real new information out there? A company press release with a tripwire on the third line, an earnings report that looks like trouble? If it relates to an investment technique you don't understand, learn more about the technique—including whether any reputable investors believe in it.

> **Red Flags**
>
> You can even get faked out by misreading your own buy case. Peter Lynch gives the example of selling a bakery and a crackers company. He'd viewed them as takeover candidates, but the takeovers never materialized. As he puts it, "I finally got bored and disposed of my shares." What he overlooked in selling was that the companies were highly profitable, one reason they were good takeover candidates in the first place.

Whatever's going on or not going on with a stock, your standard operating procedure is always to dig your buy case out of its file folder and look it over, to see whether it still makes sense. It's your fallback, your check and balance, your bastion of rationality.

That's why you always save a copy of your original buy case, and only write an updated version if you discover genuinely new information. By saving the original, you can compare it to your current thinking and see whether you're making excuses instead of reasoned decisions.

Selling Because the Stock Has Gone Up

In the best of all worlds, your stock has gone up, and you're sitting on a potential profit. What might be some reasons for selling?

Again, the big reason is when your buy case has shifted under you. This can include discovering that some of your original assumptions weren't correct. For example, say that you invested in a regional brokerage company because of their strong retail base, but it turns out that you were wrong and most of their income is being generated by proprietary trading. Even if the stock is doing okay, you may want to sell, because your original buy case is now invalid.

Here are some other reasons to sell when things still superficially look good. Note that many of these are exactly the same reasons for not buying a stock in the first place:

Things are just beginning to go wrong for the business. For a very expensive growth stock, it could just be that things are going a trifle less well. Maybe growth is slowing. Or maybe earnings aren't exceeding expectations anymore, or even beginning to disappoint. If it's a commodity, maybe market prices are beginning to falter. After you learn a given industry, you'll be able to spot its characteristic warning signs.

The P/E has gotten too high to be realistic. In other words, the stock has become overvalued.

Note that this applies even to growth stocks, which tend to have higher valuations. A good example is Coca-Cola during the late 1990s. At the end of 1997, it was selling for $67, with a P/E of 41, 50 percent higher than the market's. One justification for the high valuation was how fast the company's earnings had been growing—17 percent in 1997—yet revenue that same year had grown by less than 2 percent. In fact, Coca-Cola couldn't keep up the pace. The stock price spiked in the first half of 1998 at $89, but earnings fell that year and the next, and the stock price soon followed.

The quality of earnings is beginning to decline.
Quality of earnings is a vague term used by investment pros to describe how well reported earnings match the reality of the business. If a company has low-quality earnings, it's using a lot of accruals and aggressive accounting policies that allow it to report revenue quickly and defer expenses.

How to recognize whether the quality of earnings is declining? Check whether cash flow and sales are growing relative to earnings. For instance, if cash flow is lagging far behind, it could mean the company is using accounts receivables to pad earnings. Or if sales are great but earnings aren't, the company might be hiding an expense control problem by recognizing revenue early.

An example of fairly extreme problems with quality of earnings is the Tyco International scandal, dating from 2002. Yes, CEO L. Dennis Kozlowski resigned that year when reports surfaced he was being investigated for attempted sales-tax evasion. But just as worrisome to investors, if not more so, were problems with the conglomerate's accounting —accounting which the company itself later admitted was "aggressive" and "intended to increase reported earnings."

Wall Street has fallen in love with the stock and the CEO has become a media darling. A subset of the valuation getting too high for comfort— love, after all, is blind—and the result tends to be overinflated valuations. As for the mesmerizing CEO, refer back to the preceding chapter for a list of potential management negatives. It's not an absolute sell signal by any means, but it should increase your wariness.

A new competitor is making some inroads. If your company has been successful, it's going to attract competition; few companies enjoy monopolies for long. An old chestnut in this category is Xerox, which owned the copier market for a brief time. A newer example is Palm, which once owned the market for PDAs but has since attracted competitors like white on rice. The result will most likely be a price war which damages all participants.

The turnaround has turned around. Or the company has changed in some other equally dramatic way. For example, it was a value stock when you bought it, but no longer. What kind of stock is it now? In such cases you have to make a brand new buy case to see whether you should still own this stranger.

The stock has grown to represent too big a slice of your investing pie. Remember Chapter 5? Even if the business is still booming healthily upward, I advise that you immediately sell some of your position to increase diversification and reduce risk. To find your trigger point, think about what would happen to your finances if the company went bankrupt. For stocks where you're not an owner or manager—and where you don't have any control or inside scoop on the business—you probably don't want to risk more than 10 percent of your hard-earned assets on the competence (or lack thereof) of strangers.

Especially if you're a value investor, you may have a natural tendency to want to sell a good result too soon. Your buy case worked out exactly as planned, but you're nervous, because you can see by looking at the P/E that the stock is no longer the svelte value it once was. Can't other investors see that, too? Shouldn't you get out before anyone else notices?

The fact is, as long as the business is sound and the market still likes the stock, you usually should wait till the valuation isn't just fair, but high. That may require tolerating a certain amount of discomfort in the meantime.

As a compromise between your brain and your gut, it's often a good idea to sell just a piece of your position. That way, you get the satisfaction of locking in at least some profit, should the stock decline. At the same time, you're preserving the opportunity for further profits on your remaining position, should the price continue to go up. When it really gets high or your buy case changes, then you can sell the remainder.

The Bottom Line

As the section on dealing with taxes later in this chapter shows, it's often a good idea to hold stocks for a year to get the lower, long-term capital gains tax rate of 15%. But the fact is, some people take things farther, and let the pleasure of thwarting the taxman trump solid reasons to sell a winner. In that case, it's usually smarter to just grin and bear your tax bill. If the share price stays high, you're just delaying the inevitable. If it doesn't, you'll wish you'd sold, taxes or no.

Selling When Things Turn Ugly

Let's suppose the stock price is sinking steadily, like an exhausted swimmer who can no longer tread water. What now?

The first thing to do is try and ascertain why. For example, if the market is reacting to bad news about the company, look at your buy case to see whether you accounted for this particular problem. If in fact you did, and everything else is still on target, then your buy case is still intact, and the price drop is just a fake-out. Not only should you hold the course, you may even want to consider buying a few more shares, if you've got the stomach for it.

On the other hand, you may discover your buy case has been punctured. Maybe the stock was supposed to be a turnaround under new management, but management is now admitting they bit off more than they could chew. Maybe you underestimated the competition. In cases such as these, it's time to cut your losses and take the tax break.

And some bad news is so bad you've just got to get out. For example:

Negative earnings surprises. A Wall Street analyst once dubbed these "cockroaches," because there's never just one. Soon earnings estimates will start falling, too.

Analysts revising earnings estimates downward. See the preceding item. Analysts tend to be optimists, so if they're suddenly pessimistic, it's a bad sign.

Ethical issues cropping up. Sell immediately on the first report from a reputable source of anything wrong with the company's accounting or business practices. This one tip alone helped me avoid a huge loss on Lernout and Hauspie back in 2000. (If you remember, Lernout and Hauspie was a Belgian maker of speech recognition software. Suspicions of inflated revenues and missing cash eventually led to an SEC investigation, bankruptcy, and the delisting of the stock from the NASDAQ exchange.)

Outbreak of a price war. Price slashing to steal customers is especially dangerous during economic downturns. Sensitive industries have included automakers, long-distance telephone providers, airlines, and PC manufacturers.

A large drop in stock price that you can't explain. Sometimes the market is right, and you've missed something.

The sector as a whole is in long-term decline because of external factors. You should have accounted for any large-scale economic or demographic trends while researching your buy case—but maybe it's a new development no one else was aware of either.

Here's another tip when considering bad news. Don't stand under a falling piano just because it hasn't hit yet. In other words, it can take a long time for the full impact of bad news on a stock to develop.

A good example of a falling piano is Lucent. It was the most widely held stock on the market in December 1999, yet even that same year, some analysts had begun to raise questions about accounting policies and earnings quality. In July 2000, Lucent warned analysts that quarterly earnings would be below estimates. More earnings warnings came in October; the CEO was fired; and in November came the news the company was looking into $125 million in revenue that might have been improperly booked. By December, this had become a $679 million write-off. And that was just the beginning.

If you'd sold in July 2000 when the company first warned that earnings would be bad, you could have gotten more than $40 for your shares. If you stuck out the full two-and-a-half-year decline, however, hanging on till December 2002, your shares would have dropped to a piddly $1.25 each. That's some piano.

The Bottom Line

My worst stock ever illustrates why you should sell quickly when the news starts to deteriorate.

Remember Ames Department Stores? In late 1988, they acquired the Zayre chain of stores. The Zayre stores were mostly located in inner-city neighborhoods, but the new management decided to convert them all to Ames stores—even though Ames stores had until then been mostly located in small towns.

The change didn't go very well. In fact, sales at the converted stores collapsed. I held on way too long as the news continued to get worse, until eventually Ames filed for bankruptcy.

This is also an example of why believing management can sometimes be bad. I'd had an extensive one-on-one meeting with management prior to the merger, and decided they had a good strategy. Ha! I call this sort of thing being "seduced by management." It's a real hazard for professional analysts and fund managers, who tend to spend more time talking to management than the average small investor.

Other Potential Reasons to Sell

What other good reasons are there for selling a stock? Any of the following should have you at least considering heading for the exit:

The company has made a large acquisition. This changes your buy case almost by definition. And studies have shown that managers who spend too much on acquisitions are usually more concerned about prestige than profit.

The stock keeps you awake at night. Beyond what it's doing to you personally, this degree of tension renders you incapable of making good decisions.

You can do better with your money elsewhere. Investing is about getting the best return for a given level of risk, so keep your eyes open. Suppose you're hanging on to a value stock that's starting to plateau, and you discover an absolutely terrific growth stock. There's no reason not to switch horses if you've gotten your money's worth out of the old stock and the new stock promises a better return for about the same level of risk. Of course, you don't want to make jumping about a habit. That only leads to chasing after mirages and high trading costs.

Dealing with Taxes

Along with trading costs, taxes have a big impact on your investing results. Here are a few tips on dealing with them—some obvious, others less so.

Do try and hold your winning stocks for at least a year, to minimize the tax bite by qualifying for the federal long-term capital gains tax and its maximum rate of 15 percent. Of course, I'm talking about stocks in your taxable accounts, not any stocks you might have in nontaxable retirement accounts.

The longer you defer selling, the longer you have the chance to earn dividends and additional capital gains on the amount you would have paid in taxes. It's almost like the government is loaning you that money. On the other hand, you may want to realize gains on a stock as part of rebalancing your portfolio, and this in fact may be more important to you. I like the idea of rebalancing, so I tend to favor this latter tactic.

Remember that the amount you pay in taxes—at least under the current tax structure—is minuscule compared to what you can lose on a stock if it declines significantly in price. One of the benefits of rebalancing is that it forces you to consider selling things before they go down, rather than holding on for the wrong reasons.

Also remember that you can use short-term losses to offset the tax on short-term gains, and long-term losses to offset long-term gains. It's not an excuse to sell a stock for which your buy case is still valid, but it can take some of the sting out of jettisoning a stock whose buy case has gone bad. Timing becomes important here, of course, because it's generally best to take large capital losses and gains in the same year.

Selling Short

Throughout this book, we've been talking about buying and selling long—that is, buying a stock outright, in hopes it will go up. When it does, you sell it and take your profit.

But there's another kind of selling, called short selling. As the name implies, it's the opposite of buying or selling long. Here's how it works: Instead of actually buying a stock, you borrow it from your broker. You then sell it for whatever the current price is.

Of course, you still owe the stock to the broker who lent it to you. What you're hoping for is that the price will fall, so you can buy it for less than you sold it for. You then return it to the lender and pocket the difference. The broker, meanwhile, makes money by charging you interest on the amount of the loan.

We haven't talked about shorts before because this is a book for beginners, and short selling is definitely not something to try when you're first starting out. I mention it here in the same spirit that old-time cartographers drew monsters on the edges of their maps: here be dragons, so better to wait until you've got more experience.

The Bottom Line

> You've got to be very selective about the stocks you short. The best candidates have high valuations and fundamentals that are likely to deteriorate. But high valuations can stay high for a long time, and the market may already have factored those deteriorating fundamentals into the stock price. In sum, it's a risky game to play unless you're very good at it.

Sell Example: Google at $300

Please note that this is again just an example, chosen at the time I was putting this book together. By the time you're reading these words, the situation will undoubtedly have changed one way or the other.

As I write this, Google is trading at roughly 40 times next year's earnings. This may not seem like a big premium when compared to Microsoft at 20 times next year's earnings—especially because Google has been growing a lot faster than Microsoft.

Pretend for a moment that you bought Google soon after its initial public offering, and that you got in soon enough that you're now holding an unrealized profit—say, almost double your original investment. Whatever the case, it's time to sell.

Why? Because Google's valuation doesn't pass the rationality test. Google tends to be seen by the average investor as a technology company, but the analysts I've read agree with me that it's more of a media company. For one thing, its profits come from advertisers, just like a TV station or a newspaper. For another, its main piece of technology—the search engine—is given away free.

So does it make sense that Google's $83 billion market cap is higher than that of the top 12 newspaper publishers combined? (Go ahead and check this figure out on your own stocks database or screening tool—it's good practice. I myself used the MSN Money Investment Toolbox you'll find referenced in Appendix B.) Sure, critics contend that Google's business is very profitable, but high margins mean that competition in Google's space will only increase.

And this is not an earnings-oriented company to begin with. Look at the "Letter from the Founders" on the company's website, and you'll see statements such as the following: "Google is not a conventional company ... We will not shy away from high-risk, high-reward projects because of short term earnings pressure. Some of our past bets have gone extraordinarily well, and others have not."

Remember short selling? My recommendation is for a sell, not a short, because I'm basing it primarily on the stock's overly high valuation. If I were convinced that the fundamentals of Google's business were headed downstairs soon, I'd go for a short instead.

What to do with your money after you sell Google? You might consider swapping into newspaper companies; their stocks have been in decline and now represent good values. Yes, newspapers are experiencing competition from the Internet, but that's been going on for a long time and they're learning how to cope. For example, they've learned that their customers are willing to pay for online access. (I know I am.)

In fact, I've bought a couple of newspaper stocks myself. For example, I own *The New York Times*, partly because I'm a subscriber, but also because its national presence and brand name give it an edge in capturing online traffic.

The Least You Need to Know

- When your buy case no longer applies, it's probably time to sell.

- You can sell either slowly or quickly, depending on whether the market still likes the stock or not.

- Don't sell a winning position too hastily, especially if you're a value investor inclined toward caution. Wait until the valuation isn't just fair but high before getting out.

- If a stock has grown to represent too big a piece of your portfolio, you'll want to sell some of your shares simply to reduce your risk.

- Some bad news can be ignored, as long as you factored it into your original buy case. But other types of bad news, such as hints of fraudulent accounting practices, can't be.

- When possible, hang on to winning stocks long enough to take the 15 percent capital gains tax, rather than being taxed at your normal rate. And time the selling of your losers so as to write those losses off against your gains.

10

Taking Stock

In This Chapter

- ◆ Avoiding common mistakes
- ◆ Don't let emotions go to your wallet
- ◆ Learn from my experience
- ◆ Getting started

In real life, it's surprisingly easy to fool yourself into thinking you're making above-average decisions, when you're not. Overconfidence is a real danger, especially when you work alone.

The information in this book, along with some of the other recommended resources in Appendix B and your own ideas, will give you a chance to truly be above average. But just knowing what to do isn't enough. You have to actually do it, and that's not as easy as you might think.

This chapter is devoted to helping you outsmart your own worst instincts, by showing you where most people go wrong—and where you can go right instead. I share what research has shown us about investors' mistakes, as well as the strategies I developed as a professional to stay on course.

> **Bulls & Bears**
>
> In dealing with the entire range of investment decisions from broad-based asset allocation to issue-specific security selection, investment success requires sticking with positions made uncomfortable by their variance with popular opinion ... Only with the confidence created by a strong decision-making process can investors sell speculative excess and buy despair-driven value.
>
> —David Swensen, manager of Yale's endowment fund, in his book *Pioneering Portfolio Management: An Unconventional Approach to Institutional Investment* (Free Press, 2000)

Behavioral Finance

Over the past 25 years, a new field has developed that attempts to systematically study the ways that investor psychology affects economic decision making. Behavioral finance, as it's called, was initiated by the work of two psychology professors, Amos Tversky and Daniel Kahneman. Although Tversky died in 1996, Kahneman later won the Nobel Prize in 2002 based on their work.

The central discovery of these two psychologists was startling. In a nutshell, the pain of loss upsets us more than the pleasure of gain—even when the dollar amounts involved are equal. Subsequent studies have verified this theory, showing that all types of investors, across all markets, seek to avoid losses more than they seek to maximize gains.

Behavioral finance has evolved since, illuminating a host of irrational beliefs and behaviors that influence our investing decisions for the worse. Here are a few of them:

The hot hand fallacy. There's a tendency to attribute skill to accomplishments that are actually a matter of random chance. For example, whenever anyone from basketball players to the managers of traditional mutual funds scores better than average for longer than average, we're likely to call them geniuses rather than lucky—even though it may well be the reverse. And remember our discussion of technical analysts in Chapter 6? A practitioner of this style who enjoys a short but stunningly successful run may believe he has an approach that works—but it's far more likely that chance temporarily helped him out.

The stick-in-the-mud effect. It's usually easier to stay with whatever arrangements are in place. For example, research shows people are more likely to participate in a 401(k) plan if inclusion is automatic and you have to opt out, than if you have to actively sign up.

The framing factor. The context surrounding a decision affects how it's made. Kahneman gave an example along these lines: if asked whether they'd agree to flip a coin if heads meant they'd win $15,000 and tails meant they'd lose $10,000, most people would say no. But if asked whether they'd make an investment in their $500,000 portfolio that carried these same odds, most of these same people would say yes. In other words, investors tend to be more rational in the context of their entire portfolio than when making an isolated decision.

The self-herding instinct. Familiarity is more likely to breed comfort than contempt. In trying to make sense out of our experiences, there's a tendency to imitate previous behaviors—even if they're not applicable in the present. This can lead to some very weird decision making. MIT professor Dan Ariely described an experiment where he first asked participants for the last two digits of their Social Security number, then asked them to name the price they'd be willing to pay for certain items. The people who were willing to pay the highest prices? Those who'd just recited out loud the highest Social Security numbers. It's just easier to stick to the herd path we're traveling on than to change course to adapt to new challenges.

Mental accounting. We tend to assign money to different categories, and to place value on keeping score in each category. This can lead to irrational behavior, such as holding on to a losing stock in hopes of "getting even" on that single investment— even though your overall portfolio has been very successful. Other examples are separating income and capital, so as to avoid "dipping into capital," or keeping an investment portfolio while at the same time running a huge debit on your credit card account at horrendous interest rates.

And you thought you had everything under control! The good news: like all bad habits, the first step toward eliminating them is acknowledging their existence.

> ⚑ **Red Flags**
>
> We'd all like to think we're rational investors. So how does one explain a study showing that sentiment associated with St. Patrick's Day and the Jewish High Holy Days can affect stock prices? Or one that suggests even professional traders don't like to sell losing stocks? Or data indicating men are more active traders than women—and achieve lower returns as a result—simply because of greater overconfidence in their financial acumen? It's always a good idea to be aware of your emotions, and ask yourself if they could be affecting your decisions.

Investors Who Trade Too Much

There's also behavioral finance research suggesting that many investors trade too often. In an article published in 1999 titled "Do Investors Trade Too Much?" Professor Terrence Odean of the University of California Davis found that customers at one discount brokerage firm had what might seem to be a very peculiar rationale for stock selection: they tended to buy stocks whose prices went up or down more than the market averages.

In other words, these investors behaved as if they were chasing hot stocks that had shot up, or rushing to sell stocks that had gone down. If so, it's an example of following the "hot" or the "cold" hand. That's the sort of impulsive, short-term behavior that's easy to fall into, but that you definitely want to avoid.

How negative can the effects of overtrading be? In a paper Odean subsequently wrote with Professor Brad Barber, titled "Trading Is Hazardous to Your Wealth," they analyzed the trading habits of more than 65,000 households with accounts at a large discount broker over a 5-year period. What they found was disturbing, especially if you're an investor who likes to buy and sell with each change in the zeitgeist.

The stock returns for the average household in the study were at first "quite ordinary, on average," Odean and Barber blandly reported. Unfortunately, these were gross returns, prior to trading costs. When the costs of bid-ask spreads (remember those?) and commissions were deducted, the net returns for the average household got worse—to the point they underperformed a comparable market index by 1.1 percent annually. And when Odean and Barber adjusted the index to account for the fact that these investors tended to select riskier, higher-return value stocks, the true measure of underperformance dropped to 3.7 percent annually.

In other words, the average household in this study would have done better to invest in mutual funds and do no stock trading at all. Trading costs had done them in.

The picture got even worse when Odean and Barber looked at the 20 percent of households that traded most often. These investors traded so much that they typically turned over their entire stock portfolio more than twice a year. Predictably, trading costs hurt them even worse than the average household: they trailed the average market return by 5.5 percent annually. When Odean and Barber adjusted the market index to account for these investors' riskier stock selection, as they had for the average household, the underperformance dropped further—all the way to 10.3 percent annually.

Think about it this way: if you knew you were going to underperform a comparable market index by 10 percent annually, why would you ever become a stock picker?

My own personal experience agrees with Odean and Barber's findings. For mutual-fund managers, jumping in and out of stocks on today's news is a good way to lose money in the long run. Likewise, individual stock pickers need to keep a firm rein on their instincts and a clear eye on their buy cases.

 The Bottom Line

At the end of each year, examine your turnover and trading costs to see whether they hurt you more than you expected. It's part of disciplining yourself to get better.

Learn from My Experience

As a chief investment officer, most recently at Pioneer Investments, I was responsible for overseeing all the mutual funds in the fund family.

I learned that there's no substitute for hard work and good thinking in selecting each and every stock. The contents of this book reflect that approach. But as a manager, I also arrived at some more general rules for building good investing habits. I think you'll find them helpful.

Focus. Mutual-fund portfolio managers usually focus on a style, such as growth or value; analysts focus on a particular industry, such as toys or software. The idea is that you boost your chances of success by concentrating on a relatively narrow area. One tactic we've already discussed is honing your style—for example, growth with a tilt toward technology. But it's also essential to limit the number of stocks you'll research and own; 10 or 15 names are probably enough. I recommend keeping a list. When you've hit your limit, don't add a new stock without dropping an old one.

Individual responsibility. Group decision making tends to mean nobody's responsible if a stock goes down. I was never comfortable with that. I wanted portfolio managers and analysts to feel strongly about the stocks they owned or recommended. Likewise, as an individual investor, you'll perform better and learn faster if you hold yourself responsible for your buying and selling decisions. Pinning the blame on analysts or news stories you read is counterproductive.

Honesty. Mutual-fund managers are judged every day by investors, based on how their stock picks do. Although you don't have to tell anyone else exactly how your portfolio performs, you should be brutally honest with yourself in your weekly review sessions. It's the only way to understand how you've done, and figure out how to do better.

Ongoing education. Professional investors are always trying to find out more about the stocks they own, as well as better ways to evaluate their results. Although you can't call the CEO anytime you want, you can develop an investor's eye. Constantly be on the lookout for new facts about stocks you either own now, or might want to own down the road.

Interest. Computer geeks love code, sports freaks love games, and investors love stocks and markets. I wouldn't have gotten into the business in the first place if I didn't love the work. Everybody has a different way of describing their involvement, but I'd put it this way: if you don't get at least some fun and satisfaction from picking stocks, you probably won't be successful.

Specialized Investment Choices

As you get more involved in investing, you're likely to encounter all kinds of specialized investment choices, many with elaborate alphabet-soup acronyms. In fact, we've talked about IRAs (individual retirement accounts), ADRs (American Depository Receipts), and ETFs (exchange traded funds) and others earlier in this book.

Two more worth knowing about are real estate investment trusts (REITs) and master limited partnerships (MLPs). The first REIT was traded in 1965; the first MLP in 1981. By law, REITs and MLPs are exempt from corporate income taxes; they're also required to pass on most of their income to investors in the form of dividends or distributions.

Of the two, REITs are more common. They let you invest in commercial real estate, such as hotels, shopping centers, apartment complexes, and office space. The relatively uncommon MLPs focus exclusively on energy and natural resources companies—oil wells and coal companies, for example.

The fact that corporate taxes are eliminated and that management is required to pay out most earnings to investors can make well-run REITs and MLPs solid income producers. But it doesn't automatically make them ultra-safe. For example, after the bursting of the Internet bubble, and again after the Sept 11, 2001 terrorist attacks, dividends on many hotel REITs went down sharply because of the falloff in travel.

Although both REITs and MLPs have done well in recent years (at least as of this writing in mid-2005), you need to do careful research on both the specific company and its business area before investing, just as you would with any stock.

Getting Started

You've resolved to avoid mistakes, control your emotions, do your research, and make smart buy and sell decisions. Now for the good part ... actually starting to invest in stocks.

The more you think about it, the more often you're likely to find yourself spotting interesting companies and industries when you're reading the paper, watching TV, working, or shopping. Hey, these *Idiot's Guides* are published by a publicly traded company (Pearson PLC, the parent company of Alpha Books, which trades as an ADR in the United States). Maybe the stock is worth a look.

The other side of getting more attuned to the investment opportunities embedded in everyday life is you'll realize you don't have to act on every idea. You'll learn to use all the information around us to your advantage without getting overloaded, and begin to be able to sort out truly promising investment insights from merely interesting ones.

And you'll see that there's no rush. If you miss out on the next big thing, you can always invest in the one that's sure to follow.

Honing Your Skills

As with anything new, the first time you look at a company's financial statement or read an analyst's report is likely to be the hardest. If you've never done this kind of research before, I recommend starting simply. Focus even more sharply at the start—maybe by beginning with just one stock, and taking your time researching it. Make your buy case in full, and then move on to another.

Make sure you understand what you're looking at and keep track of where you're finding your facts. Make a step-by-step checklist if need be; you'll be repeating these steps again and again. After a while, familiarity will mean you're spending less time and mental energy getting the facts, and more time evaluating them.

Putting Resources in Place

Just as getting comfortable with doing research won't happen overnight, finding sources of information and setting up a trading account will require a fair bit of time and thought.

We've covered what to do in Chapter 4 and Chapter 7. Appendix B has more specific information—although by no means a complete list—of resources from books to discount brokers.

Remember, you don't have to do everything at once. And you may find that one step leads to another naturally, particularly as you go through the process of doing research on a stock.

Establishing a Track Record

As you find stocks, research them, and ultimately actually buy and sell, you'll begin to get comfortable with being an investor. You may figure out when investing fits into your schedule, where you like to do your research, and which information is the most useful.

You'll build a track record as an investor, and be able to objectively see how you've done—and how you can do better. Don't rush to judgment. After more than 20 years, I'm still learning from past blunders and triumphs. I hope the information in this book helps speed your learning curve, and makes investing in stocks more personally and financially rewarding.

The Least You Need to Know

- ◆ Learn about common behavioral mistakes to help avoid them: being overly averse to taking a loss, attributing the results of chance to skill, or making the same decision over and over simply out of inertia.

- ◆ Academic research has shown that trading too much can be more costly than investors may realize; stick to your buy case and build good investing habits.

- ◆ Real estate investment trusts (REITs) and master limited partnerships (MLPs) are ways of owning shares in a business with some important distinctions from common stocks.

- ◆ Stock picking gets easier with experience— especially if you concentrate on developing good research skills and good resources.

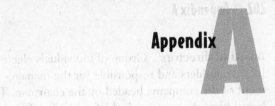

Appendix A

Stock Investing Terminology

American Depository Receipts (ADRs) A simple way of buying foreign stocks. ADRs are listed on a U.S. stock exchange, and a bank handles the foreign currency exchange for you.

asset allocation The practice of setting specific targets for diversification, designed to balance overall risk versus overall return in light of your financial goals and circumstances.

bear market A period when stock prices are falling.

behavioral finance Study of the ways that psychology affects economic decision making.

beta A way of describing how movements in a stock's price compare with those of the broader market.

bid-ask spread Difference between the highest price that any buyer is willing to pay and the lowest price that any seller is willing to receive for a share of stock. A cost of trading.

board of directors   Group of individuals elected by shareholders and responsible for the management of the company; headed by the chairman. The board hires the company's chief executive officer.

bonds   Loans made by investors to corporations or governments.

broker or brokerage firm   A financial intermediary who arranges purchases and sales of stocks. Brokers can be full service, premium discount, or deep discount.

bull market   A period when stock prices are rising.

buy case   A pithy summary of your reasons for buying a stock.

call option   A contract giving you the right (but not the obligation) to buy an asset before some future date at an agreed-upon price.

cash   Savings or money-market accounts.

commission   Payment made by an investor to a broker each time you buy or sell stocks, bonds, or mutual funds.

covered call writing   Making a *short sale* of a *call option* while you hold the underlying stock.

credit rating   An assessment of the financial health of a corporation made by one of several ratings agencies.

deep discounter   A brokerage which offers primarily trading services and little else, emphasizing low commissions. Deep discounters usually provide for trading via the Internet. See *full-service broker* by contrast.

direct purchase program, direct stock purchase plan Program that allows you to buy stock directly from a company, rather than through a broker.

diversification A way to reduce risk by placing investments in multiple assets, rather than just one.

dividend Cash payment from a company to its shareholders.

dividend reinvestment plan (DRIP) A program offered by companies that allows you to automatically reinvest your dividends in the company's stock, sometimes at a discount from the market price.

equity, equities Synonymous with *stock*, meaning a share of ownership of a corporation. The plural, equities, is often used as a term for the stock market in general.

fee-only financial planner A financial planner who charges clients a fee, usually based on assets, but doesn't earn any additional commissions from sales of financial products. Contrast to a fee-based planner, who can earn commissions in addition to a fee.

full-service broker A brokerage that offers financial advice, usually research on stocks and asset allocation recommendations, in addition to trading services. Clients are normally assigned a personal financial advisor as a direct contact with the firm. Compare to *deep discounter.*

fundamental analysis   Method of stock selection that emphasizes analysis of a company's underlying business, known as its fundamentals.

growth investor   An investor who specializes in companies that are expected to grow rapidly in the future.

index   Way of measuring the ups and downs of an entire group of stocks. Well-known indexes include the Dow Jones Industrial Average and the Standard & Poor's 500.

index fund   A mutual fund that buys shares to match a specific stock *index*.

initial public offering (IPO)   The first time a company offers stock to the public.

institutional investor   A pension fund, mutual fund, university, bank, insurance company, or other large entity that invests money for a company, non-profit, or group of investors.

intrinsic valuation   Calculation of the value of a stock derived from the cash flows generated by the underlying business.

investment bank   A financial institution that helps a company sell stock to the public.

large cap   A company with a market capitalization of more than $10 billion.

market capitalization (market cap)   Total value of all of a company's shares. Companies are often sorted according to market cap: *micro cap* (less than

$250 million), *small cap* (between $250 million and $1 billion), *mid cap* (between $1 billion and $10 billion), and *large cap* (more than $10 billion).

master limited partnership (MLP) An investment combining the tax benefits of a limited partnership with the liquidity of a publicly traded security. Available only for partnerships in energy and natural resources.

micro cap A company with a market capitalization of less than $250 million.

mid cap A company with a market capitalization of between $1 billion and $10 billion.

modern portfolio theory An economic theory that describes the role of standard deviation and correlation in portfolios.

multiples An industry term for the ratios used in relative valuation analysis, such as *price/earnings*, price-to-book value, etc.

mutual fund A company that invests in a portfolio of stocks and sells shares of the portfolio to investors. An efficient way for an individual investor to buy a large number of stocks.

premium discounter A broker providing more service than a *deep discounter*, but less personalized service than a *full-service broker*. For example, a premium discounter may offer financial advice, which a deep discounter would not, but at the cost of an additional fee.

price/earnings ratio (P/E)   The price of a company's stock divided by earnings per share for a full year. P/E can be computed using trailing (past) earnings or projected (estimated future) earnings.

put option   A contract giving you the right (but not the obligation) to sell an asset before some future date at an agreed-upon price.

quality of earnings   How well a company's reported earnings reflect the actual health of the business, as opposed to being made to look good through accounting practices.

real estate investment trust (REIT)   A method for pooling investors' capital to purchase and manage real estate (equity REITs) or mortgage loans (mortgage REITs). Like stocks, REITs are traded on exchanges.

rebalancing   Selling assets that have increased in value and buying assets that have stayed the same or gone down in value, to return an *asset allocation* to its original ratios.

Regulation F.D.   A regulation enacted by the *Securities and Exchange Commission* in 1999 to ensure that all investors get equal access to company information.

relative valuation   A calculation of the value of a stock in comparison to the valuations of other stocks.

screening Using a software tool to search a database for stocks which meet certain characteristics, such as having a low *price/earnings ratio*.

sector or market sector A group of companies in similar industries that tend to move up and down together in response to the same economic forces.

Securities and Exchange Commission (SEC)
The federal agency that regulates the financial industry, including companies that have issued stock to the public.

share A unit of stock. For example, you may want to buy 100 shares of XYZ Company's stock.

short sale, short selling Selling stock you don't own, hoping that the price will fall.

small cap A company with a market capitalization of between $250 million and $1 billion.

socially conscious investing An approach to stock selection that considers ethical issues as well as financial data.

split-adjusted Stock prices that have been adjusted for subsequent stock splits; enables the tracking of stock prices over long periods.

standard deviation A measure of volatility.

stock A share of ownership of a corporation. Synonymous with *equity*.

stock exchange   A place where shares of stock are traded—that is, bought and sold. This can be a physical location or an electronic marketplace.

stock options   The practice of giving employees, usually executives, the right to buy a certain number of shares at a preset price at some time in the future. Also called incentive or nonqualified options.

stock split   A division of shares that has no effect on overall share value. If you own 100 shares of a stock selling for $50, and it splits two for one, you'll end up owning 200 shares of a stock selling for $25 instead.

technical analysis   A method of stock selection that emphasizes analysis of market data.

ticker symbol   Abbreviation for a stock as listed on an exchange. Usually consists of one to five letters.

value investor   An investor who specializes in companies that are out of favor and trading at low prices.

volatility   The relative intensity of increases or decreases in the value or return of an investment. Stocks are considered more volatile than bonds, for example.

Further Resources

If you need the definition or explanation of a term that isn't located in this book or in its glossary, you can buy investing dictionaries, some of which are quite good. However, I find it even more convenient to go online. Two of my favorites are **www.investorwords.com** and **www.finance-glossary.com**. The rest of this resources appendix lists information on periodicals, books, and additional online resources.

Newspapers, Magazines, and Other News Sources

The Wall Street Journal. The industry standard. Also available online at www.wsj.com.

Investors Business Daily. Daily newspaper for stock junkies. Also available online at www.investors.com.

TheStreet.com, only on the web. Covers up-to-the-minute stock news.

Barron's is my top pick of the financial magazines; from the publishers of *The Wall Street Journal*. This weekly publication, with its high-quality stories on stocks and the markets, is a favorite with professionals. Also available online or through a weekly download at www.barrons.com.

Forbes is a solid biweekly business news magazine. A weekly online version is available at www. forbes.com.

Business Week provides a weekly business recap. The online version is at www.businessweek.com.

Smart Money. This monthly personal finance magazine keeps a keen eye out for investment industry folly. Like *Barron's*, published by the same company that publishes *The Wall Street Journal*. You can find some of the content online at www.smartmoney. com, including surveys of full-service and discount brokers.

Books on Investing

If newspapers, magazines, and talking heads have your own head spinning, try digging into these books. The best investment advice lasts a lot longer than the spin of the day or the week.

Picking Stocks

> *Investment Fables: Exposing the Myths of "Can't Miss" Investment Strategies,* by Aswath Damodaran; Financial Times Prentice Hall, 2004.

Graham and Dodd's Security Analysis, by Sidney Cottle, Roger F. Murray, and Frank E. Block; McGraw-Hill, fifth edition, 1988.

Money Masters of Our Time, by John Train; Collins, 2000.

Value Investing with the Masters, by Kirk Kazanjian; Prentice Hall Press, 2002.

Smart Money Stock Picker's Bible, by Nellie S. Huang and Peter Finch; Wiley, 2002.

One Up On Wall Street, by Peter Lynch with John Rothchild; Simon & Schuster, 2000.

Valuation

Investment Valuation: Tools and Techniques for Valuing Any Asset, by Aswath Damodaran; Wiley, second edition, 2002.

Technical Analysis

The Investor's Guide to Technical Analysis, by Curt Renz; McGraw-Hill, 2003.

Social Investing

Investing with Your Values, by Hall Brill, Jack A. Brill, and Cliff Feigenbaum; New Society Publishers, reprint edition, 2000.

Analyzing Financial Statements

Understanding Corporate Annual Reports, by Brian Stanko and Thomas Zeller; Wiley, 2003.

Financial Statements: A Step-by-Step Guide to Understanding and Creating Financial Reports, by Thomas Ittelson; Career Press, 1998.

The Financial Numbers Game: Detecting Creative Accounting Practices, by Charles W. Mulford and Eugene E. Comiskey; Wiley, 2002.

The Analysis and Use of Financial Statements, by Gerald I. White, Ashwinpaul C. Sondhi, and Dov Fried; Wiley, third edition, 2002.

Asset Allocation

The Intelligent Asset Allocator, by William Bernstein; McGraw-Hill, 2001.

Index Funds

A Random Walk Down Wall Street, by Burton G. Malkiel; W. W. Norton & Company, revised and updated edition, 2004.

Index Funds: Strategies for Investment Success, by Will McClatchy; Wiley, 2003.

Options

Options for the Stock Investor, by James B. Bittman; McGraw-Hill, second edition, 2005.

Characteristics and Risks of Standardized Options. The Options Clearing Corporation. www.cboe.com/LearnCenter/pdf/ characteristicsandrisks.pdf.

Miscellaneous Topics

Liar's Poker, by Michael Lewis; Penguin, 1989.

Investment Analysis and Portfolio Management, by Frank K. Reilly and Keith C. Brown; South-Western College Publishing, seventh edition, 2002.

For-Fee Databases

The first four services listed here all offer online information on companies and their stocks; all but Morningstar also offer print versions.

My top pick is Morningstar, at **www.morningstar.com.** Premium membership, currently $125 a year, offers access to analyst reports on both stocks and mutual funds. Includes screening and portfolio-tracking tools.

Hoover's, at **www.hoovers.com,** is expensive—$495 and up annually. Check to see whether your library carries it. Includes screening and portfolio-tracking tools.

Standard and Poor's Stock Reports, at **www.spoutlookonline.com.** Middling expensive at $298 per year; includes mutual-fund reports.

Then there's the database your dad might have used, at least in the print version—Value Line Investment Survey, at **www.valueline.com.** Relatively expensive at $538 annually for online access, but still highly respected. Includes screening and portfolio-tracking tools.

Miscellaneous

Want an online screening tool that's not only free, but professional caliber? Try the MSN Money Investment Toolbox, available at **www.moneycentral. msn.com/investor/controls/finderpro.asp**. It does require Internet Explorer and a Microsoft .NET passport, but those are easy to get if you don't already have them.

Want SEC filings (10-Ks, for example) for free? Visit **www.sec.gov/edgar.shtml**.

Want an actual paper stock certificate, whether as a gift or a gag? Visit OneShare at **www.oneshare. com;** they sell framed stock certificates.

Worried about whether your broker is for real? You can check their regulatory record online, courtesy of the NASD (National Association of Securities Dealers). Just go to **www.nasd.com** and look for the BrokerCheck feature.

Want to learn more about exchange traded funds? The Morningstar website at **www.morningstar. com** has an entire section devoted to ETFs, including some good educational material.

Stock Charts

Stocks charts can get expensive fast. Because you only need to take a quick look at them, see whether they're available at your library.

My top pick is Securities Research Company; they offer both 12-year and 25-year charts. These longer time periods are most useful to the fundamental analyst. Print versions only, but for more information, visit **www.srcstockcharts.com.**

For shorter-term charts (daily, weekly, and monthly), try Daily Graphs, available as hard copy or online. Visit **www.dailygraphs.com** for more information.

Stock Research and Historic Market Data

The Wall Street Transcript offers detailed interviews with Wall Street analysts, professional money managers, and company CEOs. More information is available at **www.twst.com.** Print or online versions, but both are pricey, so check your library first.

Investext offers electronic delivery of Wall Street research reports written by analysts from a variety of investment banks, brokerages, and consulting firms. Generally available only to professionals, but your library may have access.

For historic market data, try the *Stocks, Bonds, Bills and Inflation Yearbook,* published each year by Ibbotson Associates and available from booksellers, including Amazon.

For detailed information on the Dow averages, visit **www.djindexes.com.**

And for free and convenient historic stock price information, visit Yahoo! Finance at **finance. yahoo.com.**

Investment Clubs

As mentioned in Chapter 4, an investment club might be helpful if you're the sort of person who likes to bounce ideas off others rather than work by yourself.

I've never had personal experience with investing clubs, but I do know that until recently the National Association of Investment Clubs has enjoyed a reputation as one of the best—a good way to get solid information and hook up with like-minded investors.

However, that's changed somewhat. As I write this, the not-for-profit club and its parent trust are currently being sued by irate trustees, as well as being investigated by the U.S. Senate, for allegations of improper governance—among other things, excessive compensation to president and CEO Richard Holthaus.

If the allegations prove true, there's nonetheless hope for change. Judging by news reports, many members are concerned, but still support the NAIC's original mission. To learn more about the organization's goals, visit their website at **www. betterinvesting.org.**

Certified Financial Planners

Also in Chapter 4, I suggested that hiring a financial planner might be another way to have someone to talk to about stock-picking. This is true only if the financial planner actually knows something about stock-picking, however; many rely only on asset allocation. An advisor without stock-picking experience would probably want you to invest only in mutual funds, not individual stocks.

In addition, you don't want just any planner. You want one who's fee-only, meaning he or she has promised not to accept additional commissions for selling you financial products.

A good place to start in finding such a planner is the National Association of Personal Financial Advisors, which claims to be the largest professional association of fee-only financial planners in the United States. You can visit the NAPFA on the web at **www.napfa.org,** or call them at 1-800-366-2732. The website in particular provides an easy way to search for NAPFA members in your area.

Information on Socially Responsible Investing

This list is a mix of books, websites, and other sources.

As its name suggests, the **Domini 400 Social Index** is an index, similar to other stock market indices. Where the Domini index differs is that it tracks only companies that pass a variety of screens for socially responsible corporate behavior. Domini is the leader in this field, and therefore a great place to start learning. For more information on their approach, consult their website, particularly the brochure covering their standards: **www.domini. com/common/pdf/Standards_Brochure.pdf**.

KLD Research & Analytics, Inc. is the firm that originated the Domini index; it provides research on social investing issues to institutional investors. If you're got a full-service broker, your financial advisor may be able to get KLD research reports for you.

The *Christian Science Monitor* has a regular section on ethical investing, available online at **www. csmonitor.com/specials/sri**.

The basics of filing a shareholder proposal (one of the ways of engaging in socially responsible invest- ing) can be found at **www.thecorporatelibrary. com/Help/educational/Rule14a8_Filing- Shareholder-Proposals.html**.

Index

C